150

CO CEA 871

INSIDE
BENCHLEY

By
**Robert
Benchley**

Harper & Brothers
New York and London

Pictures by

GLUYAS
WILLIAMS

INSIDE BENCHLEY

Books by
ROBERT BENCHLEY

AFTER 1903—WHAT?

MY TEN YEARS IN A QUANDARY,
AND HOW THEY GREW

FROM BED TO WORSE: OR COMFORTING
THOUGHTS ABOUT THE BISON

NO POEMS: OR AROUND THE WORLD
BACKWARDS AND SIDEWAYS

PLUCK AND LUCK

THE TREASURER'S REPORT, AND OTHER
ASPECTS OF COMMUNITY SINGING

20,000 LEAGUES UNDER THE SEA, OR
DAVID COPPERFIELD

THE EARLY WORM

LOVE CONQUERS ALL

OF ALL THINGS

Table of Contents

The Social Life of the Newt

I T IS not generally known that the newt, although one of the smallest of our North American animals, has an extremely happy home-life. It is just one of those facts which never get bruited about.

Since that time I have practically lived among the newts

I first became interested in the social phenomena of newt life early in the spring of 1913, shortly after I had finished my researches in sexual differentiation among ameba. Since that time I have practically lived among newts, jotting down observations, making lantern-slides, watching them in their work and in their play (and you may rest assured that the little rogues have their play—as who does not?) until, from much lying in a research posture on my stomach, over the inclosure in which they were confined, I found myself developing what I feared might be rudimentary creepers. And

1

so, late this autumn, I stood erect and walked into my house, where I immediately set about the compilation of the notes I had made.

So much for the non-technical introduction. The remainder of this article bids fair to be fairly scientific.

In studying the more intimate phases of newt life, one is chiefly impressed with the methods by means of which the males force their attentions upon the females, with matrimony as an object. For the newt is, after all, only a newt, and has his weaknesses just as any of the rest of us. And I, for one, would not have it different. There is little enough fun in the world as it is.

The peculiar thing about a newt's courtship is its restraint. It is carried on, at all times, with a minimum distance of fifty paces (newt measure) between the male and the female. Some of the bolder males may now and then attempt to overstep the bounds of good sportsmanship and crowd in to forty-five paces, but such tactics are frowned upon by the Rules Committee. To the eye of an uninitiated observer, the pair might be dancing a few of the more open figures of the minuet.

The means employed by the males to draw the attention and win the affection of those of the opposite sex (females) are varied and extremely strategic. Until the valuable researches by Strudlehoff in 1887 (in his *"Entwickelungsmechanik"*) no one had been able to ascertain just what it was that the male newt did to make the female see anything in

2

him worth throwing herself away on. It had been observed that the most personally unattractive newt could advance to within fifty paces of a female of his acquaintance and, by some *coup d'œil*, bring her to a point where she would, in no uncertain terms, indicate her willingness to go through with the marriage ceremony at an early date.

It was Strudlehoff who discovered, after watching several thousand courting newts under a magnifying lens (questionable taste on his part, without doubt, but all is fair in pathological love) that the male, during the courting season (the season opens on the tenth of March and extends through the following February, leaving about ten days for general overhauling and redecorating), gives forth a strange, phosphorescent glow from the center of his highly colored dorsal crest, somewhat similar in effect to the flash of a diamond scarf-pin in a red necktie. This glow, according to Strudlehoff, so fascinates the female with its air of elegance and indication of wealth, that she immediately falls a victim to its lure.

But the little creature, true to her sex-instinct, does not at once give evidence that her morale has been shattered. She affects a coyness and lack of interest, by hitching herself sideways along the bottom of the aquarium, with her head turned over her right shoulder away from the swain. A trained ear might even detect her whistling in an indifferent manner.

The male, in the meantime, is flashing his

gleamer frantically two blocks away and is performing all sorts of attractive feats, calculated to bring the lady newt to terms. I have seen a male, in the stress of his handicap courtship, stand on his fore-feet, gesticulating in amorous fashion with his hind feet in the air. Franz Ingehalt, in his "Über Welt-schmerz des Newt," recounts having observed a distinct and deliberate undulation of the body, beginning with the shoulders and ending at the filament of the tail, which might well have been the origin of what is known to-day in scientific circles as "the shimmy." The object seems to be the same, except that in the case of the newt, it is the male who is the active agent.

In order to test the power of observation in the male during these manœuvers, I carefully removed the female, for whose benefit he was undulating, and put in her place, in slow succession, another (but less charming) female, a paper-weight of bronze shaped like a newt, and, finally, a common rubber eraser. From the distance at which the courtship was being carried on, the male (who was, it must be admitted, a bit near-sighted congenitally) was unable to detect the change in personnel, and continued, even in the presence of the rubber eraser, to gyrate and undulate in a most conscientious manner, still under the impression that he was making a conquest.

At last, worn out by his exertions, and disgusted at the meagerness of the reaction on the eraser, he gave a low cry of rage and despair and staggered to a nearby pan containing barley-water, from

4

which he proceeded to drink himself into a gross stupor.

Thus, little creature, did your romance end, and who shall say that its ending was one whit less tragic than that of Camille? Not I, for one. . . . In fact, the two cases are not at all analogous.

And now that we have seen how wonderfully Nature works in the fulfilment of her laws, even among her tiniest creatures, let us study for a minute a cross-section of the community-life of the newt. It is a life full of all kinds of exciting adventure, from weaving nests to crawling about in the sun and catching insect larvæ and crustaceans. The newt's day is practically never done, largely because the insect larvæ multiply three million times as fast as the newt can possibly catch and eat them. And it takes the closest kind of community teamwork in the newt colony to get things anywhere near cleaned up by nightfall.

It is early morning, and the workers are just appearing hurrying to the old log which is to be the scene of their labors. What a scampering! What a bustle! Ah, little scamperers! Ah, little bustlers! How lucky you are, and how wise! You work long hours, without pay, for the sheer love of working. An ideal existence, I'll tell the scientific world.

Over here on the right of the log are the Master Draggers. Of all the newt workers, they are the most futile, which is high praise indeed. Come, let us look closer and see what it is that they are doing.

The one in the lead is dragging a bit of gurry

5

out from the water and up over the edge into the sunlight. Following him, in single file, come the rest of the Master Draggers. They are not dragging anything, but are sort of helping the leader by crowding against him and eating little pieces out of the filament of his tail.

And now they have reached the top. The leader, by dint of much leg-work, has succeeded in dragging his prize to the ridge of the log.

The little workers, reaching the goal with their precious freight, are now giving it over to the Master Pushers, who have been waiting for them in the sun all this while. The Master Pushers' work is soon accomplished, for it consists simply in pushing the piece of gurry over the other side of the log until it falls with a splash into the water, where it is lost.

This part of their day's task finished, the tiny toilers rest, clustered together in a group, waving their heads about from side to side, as who should say: "There—that's done!" And so it *is* done, my little Master Draggers and my little Master Pushers, and *well* done, too. Would that my own work were as clean-cut and as satisfying.

And so it goes. Day in and day out, the busy army of newts go on making the world a better place in which to live. They have their little trials and tragedies, it is true, but they also have their fun, as any one can tell by looking at a logful of sleeping newts on a hot summer day.

And, after all, what more has life to offer?

"Coffee, Megg and Ilk, Please"

GIVE me any topic in current sociology, such as "The Working Classes *vs.* the Working Classes," or "Various Aspects of the Minimum Wage," and I can talk on it with considerable confidence. I have no hesitation in putting the Workingman, as such, in his place among the hewers of wood and drawers of water—a necessary adjunct to our modern life, if you will, but of little real consequence in the big events of the world.

But when I am confronted, in the flesh, by the "close up" of a workingman with any vestige of authority, however small, I immediately lose my perspective—and also my poise. I become servile, almost cringing. I feel that my modest demands on his time may, unless tactfully presented, be offensive to him and result in something, I haven't been able to analyze just what, perhaps public humiliation.

For instance, whenever I enter an elevator in a public building I am usually repeating to myself the number of the floor at which I wish to alight. The elevator man gives the impression of being a social worker, filling the job just for that day to help out the regular elevator man, and I feel that the least I can do is to show him that I know what's what. So I don't tell him my floor number as soon as I get in. Only elderly ladies do that. I keep whispering it over to myself, thinking to tell it to the world when the proper time comes. But then the big question arises—what is the proper time? If I want to get out at the eighteenth floor, should I tell him at the sixteenth or the seventeenth? I decide on the sixteenth and frame my lips to say, "Eighteen out, please." (Just why one should have to add the word "out" to the number of the floor is not clear. When you say "eighteen" the obvious construction of the phrase is that you want to get *out* at the eighteenth floor, not that you want to get *in* there or be let down through the flooring of the car at that point. However, you'll find the most sophisticated elevator riders, namely, messenger boys, always adding the word "out," and it is well to follow what the messenger boys do in such matters if you don't want to go wrong.)

So there I am, mouthing the phrase, "Eighteen out, please," as we shoot past the tenth—eleventh —twelfth—thirteenth floors. Then I begin to get panicky. Supposing that I should forget my lines! Or that I should say them too soon! Or too late! We are now at the fifteenth floor. I clear my throat. Sixteen! Hoarsely I murmur, "Eighteen out." But at the same instant a man with a cigar in his mouth bawls, "Seventeen out!" and I am not heard. The car stops at seventeen, and I step confidentially up to the elevator man and repeat, with an attempt at nonchalance, "Eighteen out, please." But just as I

*At the same instant a man with a cigar in his mouth
bawls, "Seventeen out!"*

say the words the door clangs, drowning out my
request, and we shoot up again. I make another
attempt, but have become inarticulate and succeed only in making a noise like a man strangling.
And by this time we are at the twenty-first floor
with no relief in sight. Shattered, I retire to the
back of the car and ride up to the roof and down
again, trying to look as if I worked in the building
and had to do it, however boresome it might be.
On the return trip I don't care what the elevator
man thinks of me, and tell him at every floor that
I, personally, am going to get off at the eighteenth,
no matter what any one else in the car does. I am
dictatorial enough when I am riled. It is only in
the opening rounds that I hug the ropes.

9

My timidity when dealing with minor officials strikes me first in my voice. I have any number of witnesses who will sign statements to the effect that my voice changed about twelve years ago, and that in ordinary conversation my tone, if not especially virile, is at least consistent and even. But when, for instance, I give an order at a soda fountain, if the clerk overawes me at all, my voice breaks into a yodel that makes the phrase "Coffee, egg and milk" a pretty snatch of song, but practically worthless as an order.

If the soda counter is lined with customers and the clerks so busy tearing up checks and dropping them into the toy banks that they seem to resent any call on their drink-mixing abilities, I might just as well save time and go home and shake up an egg and milk for myself, for I shall not be waited on until every one else has left the counter and they are putting the nets over the caramels for the night. I know that. I've gone through it too many times to be deceived.

For there is something about the realization that I must shout out my order ahead of some one else that absolutely inhibits my shouting powers. I will stand against the counter, fingering my ten-cent check and waiting for the clerk to come near enough for me to tell him what I want, while, in the meantime, ten or a dozen people have edged up next to me and given their orders, received their drinks and gone away. Every once in a while I catch a clerk's eye and lean forward murmuring, "Coffee"

Placing both hands on the counter, I emit what
promises to be a perfect bellow

—but that is as far as I get. Some one else has shoved his way in and shouted, "Coca-Cola," and I draw back to get out of the way of the vichy spray. (Incidentally, the men who push their way in and footfault on their orders always ask for "Coca-Cola." Somehow it seems like painting the lily for them to order a nerve tonic.)

I then decide that the thing for me to do is to speak up loud and act brazenly. So I clear my throat, and, placing both hands on the counter, emit what promises to be a perfect bellow: "COFFEE, MEGG AND ILK." This makes just about the impression you'd think it would, both on my neighbors and the clerk, especially as it is delivered in a tone which ranges from a rich barytone to a rather rasping tenor. At this I withdraw and go to the other end of the counter, where I can begin life over again with a clean slate.

Here, perhaps, I am suddenly confronted by an impatient clerk who is in a perfect frenzy to grab my check and tear it into bits to drop in his box. "What's yours?" he flings at me. I immediately lose my memory and forget what it was that I wanted. But here is a man who has a lot of people to wait on and who doubtless gets paid according to the volume of business he brings in. I have no right to interfere with his work. There is a big man edging his way beside me who is undoubtedly going to shout "Coca-Cola" in half a second. So I beat him to it and say, "Coca-Cola," which is probably the last drink in the store that I want to buy. But it is the only thing that I can remember at the moment, in spite of the fact that I have been thinking all morning how a coffee, egg and milk would taste. I suppose that one of the psychological principles of advertising is to so hammer the name of your product into the mind of the timid buyer that when he is confronted by a brusk demand for an order he can't think of anything else to say, whether he wants it or not.

This dread of offending the minor official or appearing at a disadvantage before a clerk extends even to my taking nourishment. I don't think that I have ever yet gone into a restaurant and ordered exactly what I wanted. If only the waiter would give me the card and let me alone for, say, fifteen minutes, as he does when I want to get him to bring me my check, I could work out a meal along the lines of what I like. But when he stands over me, with disgust clearly registered on his face, I order the thing I like least and consider myself lucky to get out of it with so little disgrace.

And yet I have no doubt that if one could see him in his family life the Workingman is just an ordinary person like the rest of us. He is probably not at all as we think of him in our dealings with him—a harsh, dictatorial, intolerant autocrat, but rather a kindly soul who likes nothing better than to sit by the fire with his children and read.

And he would probably be the first person to scoff at the idea that he could frighten me.

Political Parties
and Their Growth

1. *Introductory Essay*

IT WAS Taine (of "Taine Goin' to Rain No More") who said: "Democracies defeat themselves." Perhaps I haven't got that quotation right. It doesn't seem to mean much.

However, my point—and I am sure Taine's point, if he were here to make it—is that under the system of government known as a democracy, or, as it is sometimes known, the *Laissez-Faire* system (1745-1810), the ratio of increase in the population will eventually outstrip the ratio of increase in wheat production and then where will we be? Although this theory is generally credited to Malthus, I am not sure that I didn't state it before him. I certainly remember saying it when I was very young.

In writing a history of the political parties of the United States (to which this is the introductory essay and possibly the last chapter as well) one must bear constantly in mind the fact that there are two separate and distinct parties, the Republicans (a clever combination of two Latin words, *res* and *publicæ*, meaning "things of the public") and the Democrats (from the Greek *demos*, meaning something which I will look up before this goes to the

15

printer's). The trick comes in telling which is which.

During the early years of our political history the Republican Party was the Democratic Party, or, if you chose, the Democratic Party was the Republican Party. This led naturally to a lot of confusion, especially in the Democratic Party's getting the Republican Party's mail; so it was decided to call the Republicans "Democrats" and be done with it. The Federalist Party (then located at what is now the corner of Broad and Walnut streets and known as "The Swedish Nightingale") became, through the process of Natural Selection and a gradual dropping-off of its rudimentary tail, the Republican Party as we know it today. This makes, as prophesied earlier in this article, *two* parties, the Republicans and the Democrats. As a general rule, Republicans are more blonde than Democrats.

Now that we have cleared up the matter of the early confusion in names, it remains for us simply to trace the growth of the party platforms from their original sources to their present-day clearly defined and characteristic chaos. This will involve quite a bit of very dull statistical matter and talk about Inflation and Nullification, which will be enlivened by comical stories and snatches of current songs of the period. In fact, talk about Inflation and Nullification may be omitted entirely. It will also be necessary to note the rise and fall of the minor political parties, such as the Free Soil Party, the Mugwumps, the St. Louis Cardinals and Tom ("Rum-Romanism-and-Rebellion") Heflin. This

16

will not be much fun either. As a matter of fact, in outlining the subject matter of this history the thought has come to me that it shapes up as a pretty dry book and I am wondering if perhaps I haven't made a mistake in undertaking it. . . . Oh, well, we'll see.

In compiling these data and writing the book I have been aided immeasurably by the following colleagues, to whom I take this opportunity of expressing my warmest thanks (the warmest thanks on a February 9th since 1906, according to the Weather Bureau atop the Whitehall Building): B. S. Aal, Raymond Aalbue, Aalders Bros., A. C. Aalholm, Alex Aaron, the Aar-Jay Bed-Light Co., Henry W. Aarts, Theo. T. Aarup, Charles Aba, M. M. Abajian, B. Abadessa (Miss), Abbamonte & Frinchini (shoe reprng.) and Lewis Browne Zzyd.

I also wish to thank Dr. Hartmann Weydig for the loan of his interesting collection of shells, without which I would have had nothing to do when I was not writing the book. THE AUTHOR.

BIBLIOGRAPHY

"Political Parties and Their Growth, with a Key to the Calories." Robert Benchley. (Life Pub. Co.)

"Ivanhoe." Sir Walter Scott. (Ginn & Co.)

"Fifty Cocktail Recipes, with Directions for Swallowing." A. M. Herz. (Doubleday-Doran-Doubleday-Doran-Doubleday-Doran-Boom!)

"An Old-Fashioned Girl." Louisa M. Alcott. (Vir Pub. Co.)

And countless back-numbers of *Harper's Round Table*.

Call for
Mr. Kenworthy!

A GREAT many people have wondered to themselves, in print, just where the little black laundry-studs go after they have been yanked from the shirt. Others pass this by as inconsequential, but are concerned over the ultimate disposition of all the pencil stubs that are thrown away. Such futile rumination is all well enough for those who like it. As for me, give me a big, throbbing question like this: "Who are the people that one hears being paged in hotels? Are they real people or are they decoys? And if they are real people, what are they being paged for?"

Now, there's something vital to figure out. And the best of it is that it *can* be figured out by the simple process of following the page to see whether he ever finds any one.

In order that no expense should be spared, I picked out a hotel with poor service, which means that it was an expensive hotel. It was so expensive that all you could hear was the page's voice as he walked by you; his footfalls made no noise in the extra heavy Bokhara. It was just a mingling of floating voices, calling for "Mr. Bla-bla, Mr. Schwer-a-a, Mr. Twa-a-a."

Out of this wealth of experimental material I

18

Sometimes that was the only name he would call for
mile upon mile

picked a boy with a discouraged voice like Wallace Eddinger's, who seemed to be saying "I'm calling these names—because that's my job—if I wasn't calling these—I'd be calling out cash totals in an honor system lunchery—but if any one should ever answer to one of these names—I'd have a poor spell."

Allowing about fifteen feet distance between us for appearance's sake, I followed him through the lobby. He had a bunch of slips in his hand and from these he read the names of the pagees.

"Call for Mr. Kenworthy—Mr. Shriner—Mr. Bodkin—Mr. Blevitch—Mr. Kenworthy—Mr. Bodkin—Mr. Kenworthy—Mr. Shriner—call for Mr. Kenworthy—Mr. Blevitch—Mr. Kenworthy."

Mr. Kenworthy seemed to be standing about a 20 per cent better chance of being located than any of the other contestants. Probably the boy was of a romantic temperament and liked the name. Sometimes that was the only name he would call for mile upon mile. It occurred to me that perhaps Mr. Kenworthy was the only one wanted, and that the other names were just put in to make it harder, or to give body to the thing.

But when we entered the bar the youth shifted his attack. The name of Kenworthy evidently had begun to cloy. He was fed up on romance and wanted something substantial, homely, perhaps, but substantial.

So he dropped Kenworthy and called: "Mr.

Blevitch. Call for Mr. Blevitch—Mr. Shriner—Mr. Bodkin—Mr. Blevitch ——"

But even this subtle change of tactics failed to net him a customer. We had gone through the main lobby, along the narrow passage lined with young men waiting on sofas for young women who would be forty minutes late, through the grill, and now had crossed the bar, and no one had raised even an eyebrow. No wonder the boy's voice sounded discouraged.

As we went through one of the lesser dining-rooms, the dining-room that seats a lot of heavy men in business suits holding cigarettes, who lean over their plates the more confidentially to converse with their blond partners, in this dining-room the plaintive call drew fire. One of the men in business suits, who was at a table with another man and two women, lifted his head when he heard the sound of names being called.

"Boy!" he said, and waved like a traffic officer signaling, "Come!"

Eagerly the page darted forward. Perhaps this was Mr. Kenworthy! Or better yet, Mr. Blevitch.

"Anything here for Studz?" said the man in the business suit, when he was sure that enough people were listening.

"No, sir," sighed the boy. "Mr. Blevitch, Mr. Kenworthy, Mr. Shriner, Mr. Bodkin?" he suggested, hopefully.

"Naw," replied the man, and turned to his asso-

22

"Anything here for Studz?"

ciates with an air of saying: "Rotten service here —just think of it, no call for me!"

On we went again. The boy was plainly skeptical. He read his lines without feeling. The management had led him into this; all he could do was to take it with as good grace as possible.

He slid past the coat-room girl at the exit (no small accomplishment in itself) and down a corridor, disappearing through a swinging door at the end. I was in no mood to lose out on the finish after following so far, and I dashed after him.

The door led into a little alcove and another palpitating door at the opposite end showed me where he had gone. Setting my jaw for no particular reason, I pushed my way through.

At first, like the poor olive merchant in the

Arabian Nights I was blinded by the glare of lights and the glitter of glass and silver. Oh, yes, and by the snowy whiteness of the napery, too. "By the napery of the neck" wouldn't be a bad line to get off a little later in the story. I'll try it.

At any rate, it was but the work of a minute for me to realize that I had entered by a service entrance into the grand dining-room of the establishment, where, if you are not in evening dress, you are left to munch bread and butter until you starve to death and are carried out with your heels dragging, like the uncouth lout that you are. It was, if I may be allowed the phrase, a galaxy of beauty, with every one dressed up like the pictures. And I had entered 'way up front, by the orchestra.

Now, mind you, I am not ashamed of my gray suit. I like it, and my wife says that I haven't had anything so becoming for a long time. But in it I didn't check up very strong against the rest of the boys in the dining-room. As a gray suit it is above reproach. As a garment in which to appear single-handed through a trapdoor before a dining-room of well dressed Middle Westerners it was a fizzle from start to finish. Add to this the items that I had to snatch a brown soft hat from my head when I found out where I was, which caused me to drop the three evening papers I had tucked under my arm, and you will see why my up-stage entrance was the signal for the impressive raising of several dozen eyebrows, and why the captain approached

24

me just exactly as one man approaches another when he is going to throw him out.

(Blank space for insertion of "napery of neck" line, if desired. Choice optional with reader.)

I saw that anything that I might say would be used against me, and left him to read the papers I had dropped. One only lowers one's self by having words with a servitor.

Gradually I worked my way back through the swinging doors to the main corridor and rushed down to the regular entrance of the grand dining-salon, to wait there until my quarry should emerge. Suppose he should find all of his consignees in this dining-room! I could not be in at the death then, and would have to falsify my story to make any kind of ending at all. And that would never do.

Once in a while I would catch the scent, when, from the humming depths of the dining-room, I could hear a faint "Call for Mr. Kenworthy" rising above the click of the oyster shells and the soft crackling of the "potatoes Julienne" one against another. So I knew that he had not failed me, and that if I had faith and waited long enough he would come back.

And, sure enough, come back he did, and without a name lost from his list. I felt like cheering when I saw his head bobbing through the mêlée of waiters and 'bus-boys who were busy putting clean plates on the tables and then taking them off again in eight seconds to make room for more clean plates. Of all discouraging existences I can imagine none worse than that of an eternally clean plate. There can be no sense of accomplishment, no glow of duty done, in simply being placed before a man and then taken away again. It must be almost as bad as paging a man who you are sure is not in the hotel.

The futility of the thing had already got on the page's nerves, and in a savage attempt to wring a little pleasure out of the task he took to welding the names, grafting a syllable of one to a syllable of another, such as "Call for Mr. Kenbodkin—Mr. Shrineworthy—Mr. Blevitcher."

This gave us both amusement for a little while, but your combinations are limited in a thing like that, and by the time the grill was reached he was saying the names correctly and with a little more assurance.

It was in the grill that the happy event took place. Mr. Shriner, the one of whom we expected least, suddenly turned up at a table alone. He was a quiet man and not at all worked up over his unexpected honor. He signaled the boy with one hand and went on taking soup with the other, and learned, without emotion, that he was wanted on the telephone. He even made no move to leave his meal to answer the call, and when last seen he was adding pepper with one hand and taking soup with the other. I suspect that he was a "plant," or a plainclothes house detective, placed there on purpose to deceive me.

We had been to every nook of the hotel by this

time, except the writing-room, and, of course, no one would ever look there for patrons of the hotel. Seeing that the boy was about to totter, I went up and spoke to him. He continued to totter, thinking, perhaps, that I was Mr. Kenworthy, his long-lost beau-ideal. But I spoke kindly to him and offered him a piece of chocolate almond-bar, and soon, in true reporter fashion, had wormed his secret from him before he knew what I was really after.

The thing I wanted to find out was, of course, just what the average is of replies to one paging trip. So I got around it in this manner: offering him another piece of chocolate almond-bar, I said, slyly: "Just what is the average number of replies to one paging trip?"

I think that he had suspected something at first, but this question completely disarmed him, and, leaning against an elderly lady patron, he told me everything.

"Well," he said, "it's this way: sometimes I find a man, and sometimes I can go the rounds without a bite. To-night, for instance, here I've got four names and one came across. That's about the average—perhaps one in six."

I asked him why he had given Mr. Kenworthy such a handicap at the start.

A faint smile flickered across his face and then flickered back again.

"I call the names I think will be apt to hang round in the part of the hotel I'm in. Mr. Kenworthy would have to be in the dressy dining-room or in the lobby where they wait for ladies. You'd never find him in the bar or the Turkish baths. On the other hand, you'll never find a man by the name of Blevitch anywhere except in the bar. Of course, I take a chance and call every name once in so often, no matter where I am, but, on the whole, I use my own discretion."

I gave him another piece of chocolate and the address of a good bootmaker and left him. What I had heard had sobered me, and the lights and music suddenly seemed garish. It is no weak emotion to feel that you have been face to face with a mere boy whose chances of success in his work are one to six.

And I found that he had not painted the lily in too glowing terms. I followed other pages that night—some calling for "Mr. Strudel," some for "Mr. Carmickle," and one was broad-minded enough to page a "Mrs. Bemis." But they all came back with that wan look in their eyes and a break in their voices.

And each one of them was stopped by the man in the business suit in the downstairs dining-room and each time he considered it a personal affront that there wasn't a call for "Studz."

Sometime I'm going to have him paged, and when he comes out I shall untie his necktie for him.

A Romance
in Encyclopedia Land

Written After Three Hours' Browsing in a New Britannica Set

PICTURE to yourself an early spring afternoon along the banks of the river Aa, which, rising in the Teutoburger Wald, joins the Werre at Herford and is navigable as far as St. Omer.

Branching *bryophytu* spread their flat, dorsi-ventral bodies, closely applied to the sub-stratum on which they grew, and leafy carophyllaceæ twined their sepals in prodigal profusion, lending a touch of color to the scene. It was clear that nature was in preparation for her estivation.

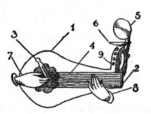

Was playing softly to himself on a double curtail or converted bass-pommer

But it was not this which attracted the eye of the young man who, walking along the phonolithic formation of the riverbank, was playing softly to himself on a double curtail, or converted bass-pommer, an octave below the single curtail and therefore identical in pitch and construction with the early *fagotto* in C.

His mind was on other things.

He was evidently of Melanochronic extraction, with the pentagonal facial angle and strong orbital ridges, but he combined with this the fine lines of a full-blooded native of Coll, where, indeed, he was born, seven miles west of Caliach Point, in Mull, and in full view of the rugged gneiss.

As he swung along, there throbbed again and again through his brain the beautiful opening paragraph of Frantisek Palacky's (1798-1876) *"Zur böhmischen Geschichtschreibung"* (Prague, 1871), written just after the author had refused a portfolio in the Pillersdorf Cabinet and had also declined to take part in the preliminary diet at Kromerice.

"If *he* could believe such things, why can not I?" murmured the young man, and crushed a ginkgo beneath his feet. Young men are often so. It is due to the elaterium of spring.

"By Ereshkigal," he swore softly to himself, "I'll do it."

No sooner had he spoken than he came suddenly out of the tangle of gymnosperms through whose leaves, needle-like and destitute of oil-glands as they were, he had been making his way, and emerged to a full view of the broad sweep of the Lake of Zug, just where the Lorze enters at its northern extremity and one and a quarter miles east of where it issues again to pursue its course toward the Reuss. Zug, at this point, is 1,368 feet above sea-level, and boasted its first steamer in 1852.

"Well," he sighed, as he gazed upon the broad area of subsidence, "if I were now an exarch, whose dignity was, at one time, intermediate between the Patriarchal and the Metropoiltan and from whose name has come that of the politico-religious party, the Exarchists, I should not be here day-dreaming. I should be far away in Footscray, a city of Bourke County, Victoria, Australia, pop. (1901) 18,301."

He came suddenly out of the tangle of gymnosperms

And as he said this his eyes filled with tears, and under his skin, brown as fustic, there spread a faint flush, such as is often formed by citrocyde, or by pyrochloric acid when acting on uncured leather.

Far down in the valley the natives were celebrating the birthday of Gambrinus, a mythical Flemish king who is credited with the first brewing of beer. The sound of their voices set in motion longitudinal sound waves, and these, traveling through the surrounding medium, met the surface separating two media and were in part reflected, traveling back from the surface into the first medium again with the velocity with which they approached it, as depicted in Fig. 10. This caused the echo for which the Lake of Zug is justly famous.

The twilight began to deepen and from far above came the twinkling signals of, first, Böotes, then Coma Berenices, followed, awhile later, by Ursa Major and her little brother, Ursa Minor.

"The stars are clear to-night," he sighed. "I wonder if they are visible from the dacite elevation on which SHE lives."

His was an untrained mind. His only school had been the Eleatic School, the contention of which was that the true explanation of things lies in the conception of a universal unity of being, or the All-ness of One.

But he knew what he liked.

In the calm light of the stars he felt as if a uban had been lifted from his heart, 5 ubans being equal to 1 quat, 6 quats to 1 ammat and 120 ammats to 1 sos.

He was free again.

Turning, he walked swiftly down into the valley, passing returning peasants with their baa-poots, and soon came in sight of the shining lamps of the small but carefully built pooroos which lined the road.

Reaching the corner he saw the village epi peering over the tree-tops, and swarms of cicada, with the toothed famoras of their anterior legs mingling in a sleepy drone, like so many cichlids. It was all very home-like to the wanderer.

Suddenly there appeared on a neighboring eminence a party of guisards, such as, during the Saturnalia, and from the Nativity till the Epiphany were accustomed to disport themselves in odd costumes; all clad in clouting, and evidently returning from taking part in the celebration.

As they drew nearer, our hero noticed a young woman in the front rank who was playing folksongs on a cromorne with a double-reed mouthpiece enclosed in an air-reservoir. In spite of the detritus wrought by the festival, there was something familiar about the buccinator of her face and her little mannerism of elevating her second

She turned like a frightened aardvark (male, greatly reduced)

33

phalanx. It struck him like the flash of a cloud highly charged by the coalescence of drops of vapor. He approached her, tenderly, reverently.

"Lange, Anne Françoise Elizabeth," he said, "I know you. You are a French actress, born in Genoa on the seventeenth of September, 1772, and you made your first appearance on the stage in *L'Ecossaise* in 1788. Your talent and your beauty gave you an enormous success in *Pamela*. It has taken me years to find you, but now we are united at last."

The girl turned like a frightened aard-vark, still

Barnaby Bernard Weenix (1777-1829)

holding the cromorne in her hand. Then she smiled.

"Weenix, Barnaby Bernard (1777-1829)," she said very slowly, "you started business as a publisher in London about 1797."

They looked at each other for a moment in silence. He was the first to speak.

"Miss Lange, Anne," he said, "let us go together to Lar—and be happy there—happy as two ais, or three-toed South American sloths."

She lowered her eyes.

"I will go with you Mr. Weenix-Barney," she said, "to the ends of the earth. But why to Lar? Why not to Wem?"

Why not to Wem? (from a contemporaneous print)

"Because," said the young man, "Lar is the capital of Laristan, in 27 degrees, 30 minutes N., 180 miles from Shiraz, and contains an old bazaar consisting of four arcades each 180 feet long."

Their eyes met, and she placed her hands in his.

And, from the woods, came the mellow whinnying of a herd of vip, the wool of which is highly valued for weaving.

Fascinating Crimes

1. The Odd Occurrence in the Life of Dr. Meethas

EARLY in the evening of October 14, 1879, Dr. Attemas Meethas, a physician of good repute in Elkhart, Indiana, went into the pantry of his home at 11 Elm Street, ostensibly to see if there was any of that cold roast pork left. The good doctor was given to nibbling cold roast pork when occasion offered.

As he passed through the living-room on his way to the pantry, he spoke to his housekeeper, Mrs. Omphrey, and said that, if everything turned out all right, he would be at that cold roast pork in about half a minute (Elkhart time—an hour earlier than Eastern time). "Look out for the pits," Mrs. Omphrey cautioned him, and went on with her stitching. Mrs. Omphrey, in her spare time, was a stitcher of uppers for the local shoe-factory.

This is the last that was seen of Dr. Attemas Meethas alive. It is doubtful if he ever even reached the pantry, for the cold roast pork was found untouched on a plate, and Dr. Meethas was found, three days later, hanging from the top of the flag-pole on the roof of the Masonic Lodge. The mystery was even more puzzling in that Dr. Meethas was not a Mason.

Citizens of Elkhart, on being grilled, admitted

The revolting death of Dr. Meethas
—Courtesy of John Held, Jr., and Life.

having seen the doctor hanging from the flag-pole
for two days, but thought that he was fooling and
would come down soon enough when he got hungry. But when, after three days, he made no sign
of descending, other than to drop off one shoe, a
committee was formed to investigate. It was found
that their fellow-citizen, far from playing a practical joke on them, had had one played on him, for
he was quite dead, with manifold and singular
abrasions. A particularly revolting feature of the

38

case was that the little gold chain which the doctor wore over his right ear, to keep his pince-nez glasses in place, was still in position. This at once disposed of the possibility of suicide.

Mrs. Omphrey and her uppers were held for examination, as it was understood that she had at one time made an attempt on the doctor's life, on the occasion of his pushing her down when they were skating together. But her story in the present affair was impregnable. After the doctor had gone through the living-room on his way to the pantry, she said that she continued stitching at her machine until nine o'clock in the evening. She thought it a little odd that Dr. Meethas did not return from the pantry, but figured it out that there was probably quite a lot of cold roast pork there and that he was still busy nibbling. At nine o'clock, however, she stopped work and started on her rounds of the house to lock up for the night. On reaching the pantry, she found that her employer was not there, and had not been there; at least that he had not touched the pork. She thought nothing of it, however, as it occurred to her that the doctor had probably remembered an engagement and had left suddenly by the pantry window in order not to worry her. So, after finishing the cold pork herself, she locked the bread-box and retired for the night. The police, on investigation, found the bread-box locked just as she had said, and so released Mrs. Omphrey.

When the news of Dr. Meethas' accident reached

La Porte, Amos W. Meethas, a brother of the victim and a respected citizen of the town, came directly to Elkhart and insisted on an investigation. He said that his brother had accumulated quite a fortune tinting postcards on the side, and was known to have this money hidden in a secret panel in the hammock which hung on the back porch. The police, guided by Mr. Amos Meethas, went to the hammock, slid the panel open and found nothing there but some old clippings telling of Dr. Meethas' confirmation in 1848. (He was a confirmed old bachelor.) This definitely established robbery as the motive for the crime. The next thing to do was to discover someone who could climb flag-poles.

Neighbors of the doctor recalled that some weeks before a young man had gone from door to door asking if anybody wanted his flag-pole climbed. He said he was working his way through college climbing flag-poles and would be grateful for any work, however small. He was remembered to have been a short youth about six feet two or three, with hair blond on one side and dark on the other. This much the neighbors agreed upon.

Working in South Bend at the time was a young man named Herman Trapp. He was apprehended by the authorities, who subsequently decided that he had no connection whatever with the tragedy.

So the strange murder of Dr. Meethas (if indeed it *was* a murder) rests to this day unsolved and forgotten, which is just as well, as it was at best a pretty dull case.

Dr. Meethas—The unfortunate victim
—Courtesy of John Held, Jr., and **Life.**

Christmas
Afternoon

Done in the Manner, if Not the Spirit, of Dickens

WHAT an afternoon! Mr. Gummidge said that, in his estimation, there never had *been* such an afternoon since the world began, a sentiment which was heartily endorsed by Mrs. Gummidge and all the little Gummidges, not to mention the relatives who had come over from Jersey for the day.

In the first place, there was the *ennui*. And such *ennui* as it was! A heavy, overpowering *ennui*, such as results from a participation in eight courses of steaming, gravied food, topping off with salted nuts which the little old spinster Gummidge from Oak Hill said she never knew when to stop eating— and true enough she didn't—a dragging, devitalizing *ennui*, which left its victims strewn about the living-room in various attitudes of prostration suggestive of those of the petrified occupants in a newly unearthed Pompeiian dwelling; an *ennui* which carried with it a retinue of yawns, snarls and thinly veiled insults, and which ended in ruptures in the clan spirit serious enough to last throughout the glad new year.

Then there were the toys! Three and a quarter

dozen toys to be divided among seven children. Surely enough, you or I might say, to satisfy the little tots. But that would be because we didn't know the tots. In came Baby Lester Gummidge, Lillian's boy, dragging an electric grain-elevator which happened to be the only toy in the entire collection which appealed to little Norman, five-year-old son of Luther, who lived in Rahway. In came curly-headed Effie in frantic and throaty disputation with Arthur, Jr., over the possession of an articulated zebra. In came Everett, bearing a mechanical negro which would no longer dance, owing to a previous forcible feeding by the baby of a marshmallow into its only available aperture. In came Fonlansbee, teeth buried in the hand of little Ormond, who bore a popular but battered remnant of what had once been the proud false-bosom of a hussar's uniform. In they all came, one after another, some crying, some snapping, some pulling, some pushing—all appealing to their respective parents for aid in their intra-mural warfare.

And the cigar smoke! Mrs. Gummidge said that she didn't mind the smoke from a good cigarette, but would they mind if she opened the windows for just a minute in order to clear the room of the heavy aroma of used cigars? Mr. Gummidge stoutly maintained that they were good cigars. His brother, George Gummidge, said that he, likewise, would say that they were. At which colloquial sally both the Gummidge brothers laughed testily,

What an afternoon!

thereby breaking the laughter record for the afternoon.

Aunt Libbie, who lived with George, remarked from the dark corner of the room that it seemed just like Sunday to her. An amendment was offered to this statement by the cousin, who was in the insurance business, stating that it was worse than Sunday. Murmurings indicative of as hearty agreement with this sentiment as their lethargy would allow came from the other members of the family circle, causing Mr. Gummidge to suggest a walk in the air to settle their dinner.

And then arose such a chorus of protestations as has seldom been heard. It was too cloudy to walk. It was too raw. It looked like snow. It looked like rain. Luther Gummidge said that he must be starting along home soon, anyway, bringing forth the acid query from Mrs. Gummidge as to whether or not he was bored. Lillian said that she felt a cold coming on, and added that something they had had for dinner must have been undercooked. And so it went, back and forth, forth and back, up and down, and in and out, until Mr. Gummidge's suggestion of a walk in the air was reduced to a tattered impossibility and the entire company glowed with ill-feeling.

In the meantime, we must not forget the children. No one else could. Aunt Libbie said that she didn't think there was anything like children to make a Christmas; to which Uncle Ray, the one with the Masonic fob, said, "No, thank God!"

Although Christmas is supposed to be the season of good cheer, you (or I, for that matter) couldn't have told, from listening to the little ones, but what it was the children's Armageddon season, when Nature had decreed that only the fittest should survive, in order that the race might be carried on by the strongest, the most predatory and those possessing the best protective coloring. Although there were constant admonitions to Fonlansbee to "Let Ormond have that whistle now; it's his," and to Arthur, Jr., not to be selfish, but to "give the kiddie-car to Effie; she's smaller than you are," the net result was always that Fonlansbee kept the whistle and Arthur, Jr., rode in permanent, albeit disputed, possession of the kiddie-car. Oh, that we mortals should set ourselves up against the inscrutable workings of Nature!

Hallo! A great deal of commotion! That was Uncle George stumbling over the electric train, which had early in the afternoon ceased to function and which had been left directly across the threshold. A great deal of crying! That was Arthur, Jr., bewailing the destruction of his already useless train, about which he had forgotten until the present moment. A great deal of recrimination! That was Arthur, Sr., and George fixing it up. And finally a great crashing! That was Baby Lester pulling over the tree on top of himself, necessitating the bringing to bear of all of Uncle Ray's knowledge of forestry to extricate him from the wreckage.

Hallo! A great deal of commotion!

And finally Mrs. Gummidge passed the Christmas candy around. Mr. Gummidge afterward admitted that this was a tactical error on the part of his spouse. I no more believe that Mrs. Gummidge thought they wanted that Christmas candy than I believe that she thought they wanted the cold turkey which she later suggested. My opinion is that she wanted to drive them home. At any rate, that is what she succeeded in doing. Such cries as there were of "Ugh! Don't let me see another thing to eat!" and "Take it away!" Then came hurried scramblings in the coat-closet for overshoes. There were the rasping sounds made by cross parents when putting wraps on children. There were insincere exhortations to "come and see us soon" and to "get together for lunch some time." And, finally, there were slammings of doors and the silence of utter exhaustion, while Mrs. Gummidge went about picking up stray sheets of wrapping paper.

And, as Tiny Tim might say in speaking of Christmas afternoon as an institution, "God help us, every one."

The Benchley-Whittier
Correspondence

OLD scandals concerning the private life of Lord Byron have been revived with the recent publication of a collection of his letters. One of the big questions seems to be: *Did Byron send Mary Shelley's letter to Mrs. R. B. Hoppner?* Everyone seems greatly excited about it.

Lest future generations be thrown into turmoil over my correspondence after I am gone, I want right now to clear up the mystery which has puzzled literary circles for over thirty years. I need hardly add that I refer to what is known as the "Benchley-Whittier Correspondence."

The big question over which both my biographers and Whittier's might possibly come to blows is this, as I understand it: *Did John Greenleaf Whittier ever receive the letters I wrote to him in the late Fall of* 1890? *If he did not, who did? And under what circumstances were they written?*

I was a very young man at the time, and Mr. Whittier was, naturally, very old. There had been a meeting of the Save-Our-Song-Birds Club in old Dane Hall (now demolished) in Cambridge, Massachusetts. Members had left their coats and hats in the check-room at the foot of the stairs (now demolished).

In passing out after a rather spirited meeting, during the course of which Mr. Whittier and Dr. Van Blarcom had opposed each other rather violently over the question of Baltimore orioles, the aged poet naturally was the first to be helped into his coat. In the general mix-up (there was considerable good-natured fooling among the members as they left, relieved as they were from the strain of the meeting) Whittier was given my hat by mistake. When I came to go, there was nothing left for me but a rather seedy gray derby with a black band, containing the initials "J. G. W." As the poet was visiting in Cambridge at the time I took opportunity next day to write the following letter to him:

Cambridge, Mass.
November 7, 1890.

Dear Mr. Whittier:

I am afraid that in the confusion following the Save-Our-Song-Birds meeting last night, you were given my hat by mistake. I have yours and will gladly exchange it if you will let me know when I may call on you.

May I not add that I am a great admirer of your verse? Have you ever tried any musical comedy lyrics? I think that I could get you in on the ground floor in the show game, as I know a young man who has written several songs which E. E. Rice has said he would like to use in his next comic opera—provided he can get words to go with them.

But we can discuss all this at our meeting, which I hope will be soon, as your hat looks like hell on me.

Yours respectfully,

ROBERT C. BENCHLEY

I am quite sure that this letter was mailed, as I find an entry in my diary of that date which reads:

"Mailed a letter to J. G. Whittier. Cloudy and cooler."

Furthermore, in a death-bed confession, some ten years later, one Mary F. Rourke, a servant employed in the house of Dr. Agassiz, with whom Whittier was bunking at the time, admitted that she herself had taken a letter, bearing my name in the corner of the envelope, to the poet at his breakfast on the following morning.

But whatever became of it after it fell into his hands, I received no reply. I waited five days, during which time I stayed in the house rather than go out wearing the Whittier gray derby. On the sixth day I wrote him again, as follows:

Cambridge, Mass.
Nov. 14, 1890.

Dear Mr. Whittier:

How about that hat of mine?

Yours respectfully,

ROBERT C. BENCHLEY

I received no answer to this letter either. Concluding that the good gray poet was either too busy or too gosh-darned mean to bother with the thing, I myself adopted an attitude of supercilious unconcern and closed the correspondence with the following terse message:

Cambridge, Mass.
December 4, 1890.

Dear Mr. Whittier:

It is my earnest wish that the hat of mine which you are keeping will slip down over your eyes some day, interfering with your vision to such an extent that you will walk off the sidewalk into the gutter and receive painful, albeit superficial, injuries.

Your young friend,

ROBERT C. BENCHLEY

Here the matter ended so far as I was concerned, and I trust that biographers in the future will not let any confusion of motives or misunderstanding of dates enter into a clear and unbiased statement of the whole affair. We must not have another Shelley-Byron scandal.

A Christmas Spectacle

For Use in Christmas Eve Entertainments in the Vestry

AT THE opening of the entertainment the Superintendent will step into the footlights, recover his balance apologetically, and say:

"Boys and girls of the Intermediate Department, parents and friends: I suppose you all know why we are here tonight. (At this point the audience will titter apprehensively.) Mrs. Drury and her class of little girls have been working very hard to make this entertainment a success, and I am sure that everyone here tonight is going to have what I overheard one of my boys the other day calling 'some good time.' (Indulgent laughter from the little boys.) And may I add before the curtain goes up that immediately after the entertainment we want you all to file out into the Christian Endeavor room, where there will be a Christmas tree, 'with all the fixin's,' as the boys say." (Shrill whistling from the little boys and immoderate applause from everyone.)

There will then be a wait of twenty-five minutes, while sounds of hammering and dropping may be heard from behind the curtains. The Boys' Club orchestra will render the "Poet and Peasant Overture" four times in succession, each time differently.

At last one side of the curtains will be drawn back; the other will catch on something and have to be released by hand; someone will whisper loudly, "Put out the lights," following which the entire house will be plunged into darkness. Amid catcalls from the little boys, the footlights will at last go on, disclosing:

The windows in the rear of the vestry rather ineffectively concealed by a group of small fir trees on standards, one of which has already fallen over, leaving exposed a corner of the map of Palestine and the list of gold-star classes for November. In the center of the stage is a larger tree, undecorated, while at the extreme left, invisible to everyone in the audience except those sitting at the extreme right, is an imitation fireplace, leaning against the wall.

Twenty-five seconds too early little Flora Rochester will prance out from the wings, uttering the first shrill notes of a song, and will have to be grabbed by eager hands and pulled back. Twenty-four seconds later the piano will begin "The Return of the Reindeer" with a powerful accent on the first note of each bar, and Flora Rochester, Lillian Mc-Nulty, Gertrude Hamingham and Martha Wrist will swirl on, dressed in white, and advance heavily into the footlights, which will go out.

There will then be an interlude while Mr. Neff, the sexton, adjusts the connection, during which the four little girls stand undecided whether to brave it out or cry. As a compromise they giggle and are herded back into the wings by Mrs. Drury, amid applause. When the lights go on again, the applause becomes deafening, and as Mr. Neff walks triumphantly away, the little boys in the audience will whistle: "There she goes, there she goes, all dressed up in her Sunday clothes!"

"The Return of the Reindeer" will be started again and the show-girls will reappear, this time more gingerly and somewhat dispirited. They will, however, sing the following, to the music of the "Ballet Pizzicato" from "Sylvia":

> *"We greet you, we greet you,*
> *On this Christmas Eve so fine.*
> *We greet you, we greet you,*
> *And wish you a good time."*

They will then turn toward the tree and Flora Rochester will advance, hanging a silver star on one of the branches, meanwhile reciting a verse, the only distinguishable words of which are: *"I am Faith so strong and pure ——"*

At the conclusion of her recitation, the star will fall off.

Lillian McNulty will then step forward and hang her star on a branch, reading her lines in clear tones:

> *"And I am Hope, a virtue great,*
> *My gift to Christmas now I make,*
> *That children and grown-ups may hope today*
> *That tomorrow will be a merry Christmas Day."*

57

The hanging of the third star will be consummated by Gertrude Hamingham, who will get as far as *"Sweet Charity I bring to place upon the tree—"* at which point the strain will become too great and she will forget the remainder. After several frantic glances toward the wings, from which Mrs. Drury is sending out whispered messages to the effect that the next line begins, *"My message bright—"* Gertrude will disappear, crying softly.

After the morale of the cast has been in some measure restored by the pianist, who, with great presence of mind, plays a few bars of "Will There Be Any Stars In My Crown?" to cover up Gertrude's exit, Martha Wrist will unleash a rope of silver tinsel from the foot of the tree, and, stringing it over the boughs as she skips around in a circle, will say, with great assurance:

> *" 'Round and 'round the tree I go,*
> *Through the holly and the snow*
> *Bringing love and Christmas cheer*
> *Through the happy year to come."*

At this point there will be a great commotion and jangling of sleigh-bells off-stage, and Mr. Creamer, rather poorly disguised as Santa Claus, will emerge from the opening in the imitation fireplace. A great popular demonstration for Mr. Creamer will follow. He will then advance to the footlights, and, rubbing his pillow and ducking his knees to denote joviality, will say thickly through his false beard:

"Well, well, well, what have we here? A lot of bad little boys and girls who aren't going to get any Christmas presents this year? (Nervous laughter from the little boys and girls.) Let me see, let me see! I have a note here from Dr. Whidden. Let's see what it says. (Reads from a paper on which there is obviously nothing written.) 'If you and the young people of the Intermediate Department will come into the Christian Endeavor room, I think we may have a little surprise for you. . . .' Well, well, well! What do you suppose it can be? (Cries of 'I know, I know!' from sophisticated ones in the audience.) Maybe it is a bottle of castor-oil! (Raucous jeers from the little boys and elaborately simulated disgust on the part of the little girls.) Well, anyway, suppose we go out and see? Now if Miss Liftnagle will oblige us with a little march on the piano, we will all form in single file ——"

At this point there will ensue a stampede toward the Christian Endeavor room, in which chairs will be broken, decorations demolished, and the protesting Mr. Creamer badly hurt.

This will bring to a close the first part of the entertainment.

"Roll
Your Own"

*Inside Points on Building and Maintaining a Private
Tennis Court*

ONE really ought to have a tennis-court of
one's own. Those at the Club are always so
full that on Saturdays and Sundays the people
waiting to play look like the gallery at a Davis Cup
match, and even when you do get located you have
two sets of balls to chase, yours and those of the
people in the next court.

The first thing is to decide among yourselves just
what kind of court it is to be. There are three
kinds: grass, clay, and corn-meal. In Maine, gravel
courts are also very popular. Father will usually
hold out for a grass court because it gives a slower
bounce to the ball and Father isn't so quick on the
bounce as he used to be. All Mother insists on is
plenty of headroom. Junior and Myrtis will want a
clay one because you can dance on a clay one in
the evening. The court as finished will be a combination grass and dirt, with a little goldenrod
late in August.

A little study will be necessary before laying out
the court. I mean you can't just go out and mark
a court by guess-work. You must first learn what

the dimensions are supposed to be and get as near to them as is humanly possible. Whereas there might be a slight margin for error in some measurements, it is absolutely essential that both sides are the same length, otherwise you might end up by lobbing back to yourself if you got very excited.

The worst place to get the dope on how to arrange a tennis-court is in the Encyclopædia Britannica. The article on TENNIS was evidently written by the Archbishop of Canterbury. It begins by explaining that in America tennis is called "court tennis." The only answer to that is, "You're a cock-eyed liar!" The whole article is like this.

The name "tennis," it says, probably comes from the French *"Tenez!"* meaning "Take it! Play!" More likely, in my opinion, it is derived from the Polish *"Tinith!"* meaning "Go on, that was *not* outside!"

During the Fourteenth Century the game was played by the highest people in France. Louis X died from a chill contracted after playing. Charles V was devoted to it, although he tried in vain to stop it as a pastime for the lower classes (the origin of the country-club); Charles VI watched it being played from the room where he was confined during his attack of insanity and Du Guesclin amused himself with it during the siege of Dinan. And, although it doesn't say so in the Encyclopædia, Robert C. Benchley, after playing for the first time in the season of 1922, was so lame under the right

61

shoulder-blade that he couldn't lift a glass to his mouth.

This fascinating historical survey of tennis goes on to say that in the reign of Henri IV the game was so popular that it was said that "there were more tennis-players in Paris than drunkards in England." The drunkards of England were so upset by this boast that they immediately started a drive for membership with the slogan, "Five thousand more drunkards by April 15, and to Hell with France!" One thing led to another until war was declared.

The net does not appear until the 17th century. Up until that time a rope, either fringed or tasseled, was stretched across the court. This probably had to be abandoned because it was so easy to crawl under it and chase your opponent. There might also have been ample opportunity for the person playing at the net or at the "rope," to catch the eye of the player directly opposite by waving his racquet high in the air and then to kick him under the rope, knocking him for a loop while the ball was being put into play in his territory. You have to watch these Frenchmen every minute.

The Encyclopædia Britannica gives fifteen lines to "Tennis in America." It says that "few tennis courts existed in America before 1880, but that now there are courts in Boston, New York, Chicago, Tuxedo and Lakewood and several other places." Everyone try hard to think now just where those other places are!

Which reminds us that one of them is going to be in your side yard where the garden used to be. After you have got the dimensions from the Encyclopædia, call up a professional tennis-court maker and get him to do the job for you. Just tell him that you want "a tennis-court."

Once it is built the fun begins. According to the arrangement, each member of the family is to have certain hours during which it belongs to them and no one else. Thus the children can play before breakfast and after breakfast until the sun gets around so that the west court is shady. Then Daddy and Mother and sprightly friends may take it over. Later in the afternoon the children have it again, and if there is any light left after dinner Daddy can take a whirl at the ball.

What actually will happen is this: Right after breakfast Roger Beeman, who lives across the street and who is home for the summer with a couple of college friends who are just dandy looking, will come over and ask if they may use the court until someone wants it. They will let Myrtis play with them and perhaps Myrtis' girl-chum from Westover. They will play five sets, running into scores like 19-17, and at lunch time will make plans for a ride into the country for the afternoon. Daddy will stick around in the offing all dressed up in his tennis-clothes waiting to play with Uncle Ted, but somehow or other every time he approaches the court the young people will be in the middle of a set.

After lunch, Lillian Nieman, who lives three houses down the street, will come up and ask if she may bring her cousin (just on from the West) to play a set until someone wants the court. Lillian's cousin has never played tennis before but she has done a lot of croquet and thinks she ought to pick tennis up rather easily. For three hours there is a great deal of screaming, with Lillian and her cousin hitting the ball an aggregate of eleven times, while Daddy patters up and down the side-lines, all dressed up in white, practising shots against the netting.

Finally, the girls will ask him to play with them, and he will thank them and say that he has to go in the house now as he is all perspiration and is afraid of catching cold.

After dinner there is dancing on the court by the young people. Anyway, Daddy is getting pretty old for tennis.

Opera Synopses

Some Sample Outlines of Grand Opera Plots For Home Study

I

DIE MEISTER-GENOSSENSCHAFT

SCENE: *The Forests of Germany.*
TIME: *Antiquity.*

CAST

STRUDEL, *God of Rain* . . . . Basso
SCHMALZ, *God of Slight Drizzle* . . . . Tenor
IMMERGLÜCK, *Goddess of the Six Primary Colors* . . . . Soprano
LUDWIG DAS EIWEISS, *the Knight of the Iron Duck* . . . . Baritone
THE WOODPECKER . . . . Soprano

ARGUMENT

The basis of "Die Meister-Genossenschaft" is an old legend of Germany which tells how the Whale got his Stomach.

ACT 1

The Rhine at Low Tide Just Below Weldschnoffen.—Immerglück has grown weary of always sitting on the same rock with the same fishes swimming by every day, and sends for Schwül to suggest

65

something to do. Schwül asks her how she would like to have pass before her all the wonders of the world fashioned by the hand of man. She says, rotten. He then suggests that Ringblattz, son of Pflucht, be made to appear before her and fight a mortal combat with the Iron Duck. This pleases Immerglück and she summons to her the four dwarfs: Hot Water, Cold Water, Cool, and Cloudy. She bids them bring Ringblattz to her. They refuse, because Pflucht has at one time rescued them from being buried alive by acorns, and, in a rage, Immerglück strikes them all dead with a thunderbolt.

ACT 2

A Mountain Pass.—Repenting of her deed, Immerglück has sought advice of the giants, Offen and Besitz, and they tell her that she must procure the magic zither which confers upon its owner the power to go to sleep while apparently carrying on a conversation. This magic zither has been hidden for three hundred centuries in an old bureau drawer, guarded by the Iron Duck, and, although many have attempted to rescue it, all have died of a strange ailment just as success was within their grasp.

But Immerglück calls to her side Dampfboot, the tinsmith of the gods, and bids him make for her a tarnhelm or invisible cap which will enable her to talk to people without their understanding a word she says. For a dollar and a half extra Dampf-boot throws in a magic ring which renders its wearer insensible. Thus armed, Immerglück starts out for Walhalla, humming to herself.

ACT 3

The Forest Before the Iron Duck's Bureau Drawer.—Merglitz, who has up till this time held his peace, now descends from a balloon and demands the release of Betty. It has been the will of Wotan that Merglitz and Betty should meet on earth and hate each other like poison, but Zwei-back, the druggist of the gods, has disobeyed and concocted a love-potion which has rendered the young couple very unpleasant company. Wotan, enraged, destroys them with a protracted heat spell.

Encouraged by this sudden turn of affairs, Immerglück comes to earth in a boat drawn by four white Holsteins, and, seated alone on a rock, remembers aloud to herself the days when she was a girl. Pilgrims from Augenblick, on their way to worship at the shrine of Schmürr, hear the sound of reminiscence coming from the rock and stop in their march to sing a hymn of praise for the drying up of the crops. They do not recognize Immerglück, as she has her hair done differently, and think that she is a beggar girl selling pencils.

In the meantime, Ragel, the papercutter of the gods, has fashioned himself a sword on the forge of Schmalz, and has called the weapon "Assistance-in-Emergency." Armed with Assistance-in-Emergency" he comes to earth, determined to slay the Iron Duck and carry off the beautiful Irma.

But Frimsel overhears the plan and has a drink brewed which is given to Ragel in a golden goblet and which, when drunk, makes him forget his past and causes him to believe that he is Schnorr, the God of Fun. While laboring under this spell, Ragel has a funeral pyre built on the summit of a high mountain and, after lighting it, climbs on top of it with a mandolin which he plays until he is consumed.

Immerglück never marries.

II

IL MINNESTRONE
(Peasant Love)

Scene: *Venice and Old Point Comfort.*
Time: *Early 16th Century.*

Cast

Alfonso, *Duke of Minnestrone*.......		Baritone
Partola, *a Peasant Girl*		*Soprano*
Cleanso		Tenor
Turino	*Young Noblemen of Venice.*	Tenor
Bombo		Basso
Ludovico	*Assassins in the service of*	Basso
Astolfo	*Cafeteria Rusticana*	Methodist

Townspeople, Cabbies and Sparrows

68

ARGUMENT

"Il Minnestrone" is an allegory of the two sides of a man's nature (good and bad), ending at last in an awfully comical mess with everyone dead.

ACT 1

A Public Square, Ferrara.—During a peasant festival held to celebrate the sixth consecutive day of rain, Rudolpho, a young nobleman, sees Lilliano, daughter of the village bell-ringer, dancing along throwing artificial roses at herself. He asks of his secretary who the young woman is, and his secretary, in order to confuse Rudolpho and thereby win the hand of his ward, tells him that it is his (Rudolpho's) own mother, disguised for the festival. Rudolpho is astounded. He orders her arrest.

ACT 2

Banquet Hall in Gorgio's Palace.—Lilliano has not forgotten Breda, her old nurse, in spite of her troubles, and determines to avenge herself for the many insults she received in her youth by poisoning her (Breda). She therefore invites the old nurse to a banquet and poisons her. Presently a knock is heard. It is Ugolfo. He has come to carry away the body of Michelo and to leave an extra quart of pasteurized. Lilliano tells him that she no longer loves him, at which he goes away, dragging his feet sulkily.

Act 3

In Front of Emilo's House.—Still thinking of the old man's curse, Borsa has an interview with Cleanso, believing him to be the Duke's wife. He tells him things can't go on as they are, and Cleanso stabs him. Just at this moment Betty comes rushing in from school and falls in a faint. Her worst fears have been realized. She has been insulted by Sigmundo, and presently dies of old age. In a fury, Ugolfo rushes out to kill Sigmundo and, as he does so, the dying Rosenblatt rises on one elbow and curses his mother.

III

LUCY DE LIMA

SCENE: *Wales.*
TIME: *1700 (Greenwich).*

CAST

WILLIAM WONT, *Lord of Glennnn* . . . . Basso
LUCY WAGSTAFF, *his daughter* . . . . Soprano
BERTRAM, *her lover* . . . . Tenor
LORD ROGER, *friend of Bertram* . . . . Soprano
IRMA, *attendant to Lucy* . . . . Basso
*Friends, Retainers and Members of the local
Lodge of Elks.*

ARGUMENT

"Lucy de Lima," is founded on the well-known story by Boccaccio of the same name and address.

70

ACT 1

Gypsy Camp Near Waterbury.—The gypsies, led by Edith, go singing through the camp on the way to the fair. Following them comes Despard, the gypsy leader, carrying Ethel, whom he has just kidnapped from her father, who had previously just kidnapped her from her mother. Despard places Ethel on the ground and tells Mona, the old hag, to watch over her. Mona nurses a secret grudge against Despard for having once cut off her leg and decides to change Ethel for Nettie, another kidnapped child. Ethel pleads with Mona to let her stay with Despard, for she has fallen in love with him on the ride over. But Mona is obdurate.

ACT 2

The Fair.—A crowd of sightseers and villagers is present. Roger appears, looking for Laura. He can not find her. Laura appears, looking for Roger. She can not find him. The gypsy queen approaches Roger and thrusts into his hand the locket stolen from Lord Brym. Roger looks at it and is frozen with astonishment, for it contains the portrait of his mother when she was in high school. He then realizes that Laura must be his sister, and starts out to find her.

ACT 3

Hall in the Castle.—Lucy is seen surrounded by every luxury, but her heart is sad. She has just been

71

shown a forged letter from Stewart saying that he no longer loves her, and she remembers her old free life in the mountains and longs for another romp with Ravensbane and Wolfshead, her old pair of rompers. The guests begin to assemble for the wedding, each bringing a roast ox. They chide Lucy for not having her dress changed. Just at this moment the gypsy band bursts in and Cleon tells the wedding party that Elsie and not Edith is the child who was stolen from the summer-house, showing the blood-stained derby as proof. At this, Lord Brym repents and gives his blessing on the pair, while the fishermen and their wives celebrate in the courtyard.

The Tooth, the Whole Tooth, and Nothing but the Tooth

SOME well-known saying (it doesn't make much difference what) is proved by the fact that everyone likes to talk about his experiences at the dentist's. For years and years little articles like this have been written on the subject, little jokes like some that I shall presently make have been made, and people in general have been telling other people just what emotions they experience when they crawl into the old red plush guillotine.

They like to explain to each other how they feel when the dentist puts "that buzzer thing" against their bicuspids, and, if sufficiently pressed, they will describe their sensations on mouthing a rubber dam.

"I'll tell you what I hate," they will say with great relish, "when he takes that little nut-pick and begins to scrape. Ugh!"

"Oh, I'll tell you what's worse than that," says the friend, not to be outdone, "when he is poking around careless-like, and strikes a nerve. Wow!"

And if there are more than two people at the experience-meeting, everyone will chip in and tell what he or she considers to be the worst phase of the dentist's work, all present enjoying the narration hugely and none so much as the narrator who has suffered so.

This sort of thing has been going on ever since the first mammoth gold tooth was hung out as a bait to folks in search of a good time. (By the way, when *did* the present obnoxious system of dentistry begin? It can't be so very long ago that the electric auger was invented, and where would a dentist be without an electric auger? Yet you never hear of Amalgam Filling Day, or any other anniversary in the dental year. There must be a conspiracy of silence on the part of the trade to keep hidden the names of the men who are responsible for all this.)

However many years it may be that dentists have been plying their trade, in all that time people have never tired of talking about their teeth. This is probably due to the inscrutable workings of Nature who is always supplying new teeth to talk about.

As a matter of fact, the actual time and suffering in the chair is only a fraction of the gross expenditure connected with the affair. The preliminary period, about which nobody talks, is much the worse. This dates from the discovery of the wayward tooth and extends to the moment when the dentist places his foot on the automatic hoist which jacks you up into range. Giving gas for tooth-extraction is all very humane in its way, but the time for anaesthetics is when the patient first decides that he must go to the dentist. From then on, until the first excavation is started, should be shrouded in oblivion.

There is probably no moment more appalling

than that in which the tongue, running idly over the teeth in a moment of care-free play, comes suddenly upon the ragged edge of a space from which the old familiar filling has disappeared. The world stops and you look meditatively up to the corner of the ceiling. Then quickly you draw your tongue away, and try to laugh the affair off, saying to yourself:

"Stuff and nonsense, my good fellow! There is nothing the matter with your tooth. Your nerves are upset after a hard day's work, that's all."

Having decided this to your satisfaction, you slyly, and with a poor attempt at being casual, slide the tongue back along the line of adjacent teeth, hoping against hope that it will reach the end without mishap.

But there it is! There can be no doubt about it this time. The tooth simply has got to be filled by someone, and the only person who can fill it with anything permanent is a dentist. You wonder if you might not be able to patch it up yourself for the time being,—a year or so—perhaps with a little spruce-gum and a coating of new-skin. It is fairly far back, and wouldn't have to be a very sightly job.

But this has an impracticable sound, even to you. You might want to eat some peanut-brittle (you never can tell when someone might offer you peanut-brittle these days), and the new-skin, while serviceable enough in the case of cream soups and custards, couldn't be expected to stand up under heavy crunching.

So you admit that, since the thing has got to be filled, it might as well be a dentist who does the job.

This much decided, all that is necessary is to call him up and make an appointment.

Let us say that this resolve is made on Tuesday. That afternoon you start to look up the dentist's number in the telephone-book. A great wave of relief sweeps over you when you discover that it isn't there. How can you be expected to make an appointment with a man who hasn't got a telephone? And how can you have a tooth filled without making an appointment? The whole thing is impossible, and that's all there is to it. God knows you did your best.

On Wednesday there is a slightly more insistent twinge, owing to bad management of a sip of ice-water. You decide that you simply must get in touch with that dentist when you get back from lunch. But you know how those things are. First one thing and then another came up, and a man came in from Providence who had to be shown around the office, and by the time you had a minute to yourself it was five o'clock. And, anyway, the tooth didn't bother you again. You wouldn't be surprised if, by being careful, you could get along with it as it is until the end of the week when you will have more time. A man has to think of his business, after all, and what is a little personal discomfort in the shape of an unfilled tooth to the satisfaction of work well done in the office?

By Saturday morning you are fairly reconciled to going ahead, but it is only a half day and probably he has no appointments left, anyway. Monday is really the time. You can begin the week afresh. After all, Monday is really the logical day to start in going to the dentist.

Bright and early Monday morning you make another try at the telephone-book, and find, to your horror, that some time between now and last Tuesday the dentist's name and number have been inserted into the directory. There it is. There is no getting around it: "Burgess, Jas. Kendal, DDS. . . . Courtland—2654." There is really nothing left to do but to call him up. Fortunately the line is busy, which gives you a perfectly good excuse for putting it over until Tuesday. But on Tuesday luck is against you and you get a clear connection with the doctor himself. An appointment is arranged for Thursday afternoon at 3:30.

Thursday afternoon, and here it is only Tuesday morning! Almost anything may happen between now and then. We might declare war on Mexico, and off you'd have to go, dentist appointment or no dentist appointment. Surely a man couldn't let a date to have a tooth filled stand in the way of his doing his duty to his country. Or the social revolution might start on Wednesday, and by Thursday the whole town might be in ashes. You can picture yourself standing, Thursday afternoon at 3:30, on the ruins of the City Hall, fighting off marauding bands of reds, and saying to yourself, with a sigh of relief: "Only to think! At this time I was to have been climbing into the dentist's chair!" You never can tell when your luck will turn in a thing like that.

But Wednesday goes by and nothing happens. And Thursday morning dawns without even a word from the dentist saying that he has been called suddenly out of town to lecture before the Incisor Club. Apparently, everything is working against you.

By this time, your tongue has taken up a permanent resting-place in the vacant tooth, and is causing you to talk indistinctly and incoherently. Somehow you feel that if the dentist opens your mouth and finds the tip of your tongue in the tooth, he will be deceived and go away without doing anything.

The only thing left is for you to call him up and say that you have just killed a man and are being arrested and can't possibly keep your appointment. But any dentist would see through that. He would laugh right into his transmitter at you. There is probably no excuse which it would be possible to invent which a dentist has not already heard eighty or ninety times. No, you might as well see the thing through now.

Luncheon is a ghastly rite. The whole left side of your jaw has suddenly developed an acute sensitiveness and the disaffection has spread to the four teeth on either side of the original one. You doubt if it will be possible for him to touch it at all. Perhaps all he intends to do this time is to look at it anyway. You might even suggest that to him. You could very easily come in again soon and have him do the actual work.

Three-thirty draws near. A horrible time of day at best. Just when a man's vitality is lowest. Before stepping in out of the sunlight into the building in which the dental parlor is, you take one look about you at the happy people scurrying by in the street. Carefree children that they are! What do they know of Life? Probably that man in the silly-looking hat never had trouble with so much as his baby-teeth. There they go, pushing and jostling each other, just as if within ten feet of them there was not a man who stands on the brink of the Great Misadventure. Ah well! Life is like that!

Into the elevator. The last hope is gone. The door clangs and you look hopelessly about you at the stupid faces of your fellow passengers. How can people be so clownish? Of course, there is always the chance that the elevator will fall and that you will all be terribly hurt. But that is too much to expect. You dismiss it from your thoughts as too impractical, too visionary. Things don't work out as happily as that in real life.

You feel a certain glow of heroic pride when you tell the operator the right floor number. You might just as easily have told him a floor too high or too low, and that would, at least, have caused delay. But after all, a man must prove himself a man and the least you can do is to meet Fate with an unflinching eye and give the right floor number.

Too often has the scene in the dentist's waiting-room been described for me to try to do it again here. They are all alike. The antiseptic smell, the ominous hum from the operating-rooms, the ancient *Digests,* and the silent, sullen group of waiting patients, each trying to look unconcerned and cordially disliking everyone else in the room, —all these have been sung by poets of far greater lyric powers than mine. (Not that I really think that they *are* greater than mine, but that's the customary form of excuse for not writing something you haven't got time or space to do. As a matter of fact, I think I could do it much better than it has ever been done before).

I can only say that, as you sit looking, with unseeing eyes, through a large book entitled, "The War in Pictures," you would gladly change places with the most lowly of God's creatures. It is inconceivable that there should be anyone worse off than you, unless perhaps it is some of the poor wretches who are waiting with you.

That one over in the arm-chair, nervously tearing to shreds a copy of "The Dental Review and Practical Inlay Worker." She may have something frightful the trouble with her. She couldn't possibly look more worried. Perhaps it is very, very painful. This thought cheers you up considerably. What cowards women are in times like these!

And then there comes the sound of voices from the next room.

"All right, Doctor, and if it gives me any more pain shall I call you up? . . . Do you think that it will bleed much more? . . . Saturday morning, then, at eleven. . . . Good bye, Doctor."

And a middle-aged woman emerges (all women are middle-aged when emerging from the dentist's office) looking as if she were playing the big emotional scene in "John Ferguson." A wisp of hair waves dissolutely across her forehead between her eyes. Her face is pale, except for a slight inflammation at the corners of her mouth, and in her eyes is that far-away look of one who has been face to face with Life. But she is through. She should care how she looks.

The nurse appears, and looks inquiringly at each one in the room. Each one in the room evades the nurse's glance in one last, futile attempt to fool someone and get away without seeing the dentist. But she spots you and nods pleasantly. God, how pleasantly she nods! There ought to be a law against people being as pleasant as that.

"The doctor will see you now," she says.

The English language may hold a more disagreeable combination of words than "The doctor will see you now." I am willing to concede something to the phrase "Have you anything to say before the current is turned on." That may be worse for the

81

moment, but it doesn't last so long. For continued, unmitigating depression, I know nothing to equal "The doctor will see you now." But I'm not narrow-minded about it. I'm willing to consider other possibilities.

Smiling feebly, you trip over the extended feet of the man next to you, and stagger into the delivery-room, where amid a ghastly array of death-masks of teeth, blue flames waving eerily from Bunsen burners, and the drowning sound of perpetually running water which chokes and gurgles at intervals, you sink into the chair and close your eyes.

．　．　．　．　．　．

But now let us consider the spiritual exaltation that comes when you are at last let down and turned loose. It is all over, and what did it amount to? Why, nothing at all. A-ha-ha-ha-ha-ha! Nothing at all.

You suddenly develop a particular friendship for the dentist. A splendid fellow, really. You ask him questions about his instruments. What does he use this thing for, for instance? Well, well, to think of a little thing like that making all that trouble. A-ha-ha-ha-ha-ha! . . . And the dentist's family, how are they? Isn't that fine!

Gaily you shake hands with him and straighten your tie. Forgotten is the fact that you have another appointment with him for Monday. There is no such thing as Monday. You are through for today, and all's right with the world.

As you pass out through the waiting-room, you leer at the others unpleasantly. The poor fishes! Why can't they take their medicine like grown people and not sit there moping as if they were going to be shot?

Heigh-ho! Here's the elevator-man! A charming fellow! You wonder if he knows that you have just had a tooth filled. You feel tempted to tell him and slap him on the back. You feel tempted to tell everyone out in the bright, cheery street. And what a wonderful street it is too! All full of nice, black snow and water. After all, Life is sweet!

And then you go and find the first person whom you can accost without being arrested and explain to him just what it was that the dentist did to you, and how you felt, and what you have got to have done next time.

Which brings us right back to where we were in the beginning, and perhaps accounts for everyone's liking to divulge their dental secrets to others. It may be a sort of hysterical relief that, for the time being, it is all over with.

Literary Lost and Found Department

With Scant Apology to the Book Section of the
New York Times

"Old Black Tillie"

H.G.L.—When I was a little girl, my nurse used to recite a poem something like the following (as near as I can remember). I wonder if anyone can give me the missing lines?

> *"Old Black Tillie lived in the dell,*
> *Heigh-ho with a rum-tum-tum!*
> *Something, something, something like a lot of hell,*
> *Heigh-ho with a rum-tum-tum!*
> *She wasn't very something and she wasn't very fat*
> *But ——"*

"Victor Hugo's Death"

M.K.C.—Is it true that Victor Hugo did not die but is still living in a little shack in Colorado?

"I'm Sorry That I Spelt the Word"

J.R.A.—Can anyone help me out by furnishing the last three words to the following stanza which I learned in school and of which I have forgotten the last three words, thereby driving myself crazy?

> "'I'm sorry that I spelt the word,
> I hate to go above you,
> Because—' the brown eyes lower fell,
> 'Because, you see, — — —.'"

"God's in His Heaven"

J.A.E.—Where did Mark Twain write the following?

> "God's in his heaven:
> All's right with the world."

"She Dwelt Beside"

N.K.Y.—Can someone locate this for me and tell the author?

> "She dwelt among untrodden ways,
> Beside the springs of Dove,
> To me she gave sweet Charity,
> But greater far is Love."

"The Golden Wedding"

K.L.F.—Who wrote the following and what does it mean?

> "Oh, de golden wedding,
> Oh, de golden wedding,
> Oh, de golden wedding,
> De golden, golden wedding!"

ANSWERS

"WHEN GRANDMA WAS A GIRL"

LUTHER F. NEAM, Flushing, L. I.—The poem asked for by "E.J.K." was recited at a Free Soil riot in Ashburg, Kansas, in July, 1850. It was entitled, "And That's the Way They Did It When Grandma Was a Girl," and was written by Bishop Leander B. Rizzard. The last line runs:

"And that's the way they did it, when Grandma was a
girl."

Others who answered this query were: Lillian W. East, of Albany; Martin B. Forsch, New York City, and Henry Cabot Lodge, Nahant.

"LET US THEN BE UP AND DOING"

ROGER F. NILKETTE, Presto, N. J.—Replying to the query in your last issue concerning the origin of the lines:

"Let us then be up and doing,
With a heart for any fate.
Still achieving, still pursuing,
Learn to labor and to wait."

I remember hearing these lines read at a gathering in the Second Baptist Church of Presto, N. J., when I was a young man, by the Reverend Harley N. Ankle. It was said at the time among his parishioners that he himself wrote them and on being questioned on the matter he did not deny it, simply smiling and saying, "I'm glad if you liked them." They were henceforth known in Presto as "Dr. Ankle's verse" and were set to music and sung at his funeral.

"THE DECEMBER BRIDE, OR OLD ROBIN"

CHARLES B. RENNIT, Boston, N. H.—The whole poem wanted by "H.J.O." is as follows, and appeared in *Hostetter's Annual* in 1843.

1

*" 'Twas in the bleak December that I took her for my
    bride;
How well do I remember how she fluttered by my
    side;
My Nellie dear, it was not long before you up and
    died,
And they buried her at eight-thirty in the morning.*

2

*"Oh, do not tell me of the charms of maidens far and
    near,
Their charming ways and manners I do not care to
    hear,
For Lucy dear was to me so very, very dear,
And they buried her at eight-thirty in the morning.*

3

*"Then it's merrily, merrily, merrily, whoa!
To the old gray church they come and go,*

Some to be married and some to be buried,
And old Robin has gone for the mail."

"THE OLD KING'S JOKE"

F. J. BRUFF, Hammick, Conn.—In a recent issue of your paper, Lillian F. Grothman asked for the remainder of a poem which began: *"The King of Sweden made a joke, ha, ha!"*

I can furnish all of this poem, having written it myself, for which I was expelled from St. Domino's School in 1895. If Miss Grothman will meet me in the green room at the Biltmore for tea on Wednesday next at 4:30, she will be supplied with the missing words.

Trout
Fishing

I NEVER knew very much about trout-fishing anyway, and I certainly had no inkling that a trout-fisher had to be so deceitful until I read "Trout-Fishing in Brooks," by G. Garrow-Green. The thing is appalling. Evidently the sport is nothing but a constant series of compromises with one's better nature, what with sneaking about pretending to be something that one is not, trying to fool the fish into thinking one thing when just the reverse is true, and in general behaving in an underhanded and tricky manner throughout the day.

The very first and evidently the most important exhortation in the book is, "Whatever you do, keep out of sight of the fish." Is that open and above-board? Is it honorable?

"Trout invariably lie in running water with their noses pointed against the current, and therefore whatever general chance of concealment there may be rests in fishing from behind them. The moral is that the brook-angler must both walk and fish upstream."

It seems as if a lot of trouble might be saved the fisherman, in case he really didn't want to walk upstream but had to get to some point downstream before 6 o'clock, to adopt some disguise which would deceive the fish into thinking that he had no intention of catching them anyway. A pair of blue glasses and a cane would give the effect of the wearer being blind and harmless, and could be thrown aside very quickly when the time came to show one's self in one's true colors to the fish. If there were two anglers they might talk in loud tones about their dislike for fish in any form, and then, when the trout were quite reassured and swimming close to the bank they could suddenly be shot with a pistol.

But a little further on comes a suggestion for a much more elaborate bit of subterfuge.

The author says that in the early season trout are often engaged with larvæ at the bottom and do not show on the surface. It is then a good plan, he says, to sink the flies well, moving in short jerks to imitate nymphs.

You can see that imitating a nymph will call for a lot of rehearsing, but I doubt very much if moving in short jerks is the way in which to go about it. I have never actually seen a nymph, though if I had I should not be likely to admit it, and I can think of no possible way in which I could give an adequate illusion of being one myself. Even the most stupid of trout could easily divine that I was masquerading, and then the question would immediately arise in his mind: "If he is not a nymph, then what is his object in going about like that try-

90

ing to imitate one? He is up to no good, I'll be bound."

And crash! away would go the trout before I could put my clothes back on.

There is an interesting note on the care and feeding of worms on page 67. One hundred and fifty worms are placed in a tin and allowed to work their way down into packed moss.

"A little fresh milk poured in occasionally is sufficient food," writes Mr. Garrow-Green, in the style of Dr. Holt. "So disposed, the worms soon become bright, lively and tough."

It is easy to understand why one should want to have bright worms, so long as they don't know that they are bright and try to show off before company, but why deliberately set out to make them tough? Good manners they may not be expected to acquire, but a worm with a cultivated vulgarity sounds intolerable. Imagine 150 very tough worms all crowded together in one tin! "Canaille" is the only word to describe it.

I suppose that it is my ignorance of fishing parlance which makes the following sentence a bit hazy:

"Much has been written about bringing a fish downstream to help drown it, as no doubt it does; still, this is often impracticable."

I can think of nothing more impracticable than trying to drown a fish under any conditions, upstream or down, but I suppose that Mr. Garrow-Green knows what he is talking about.

And in at least one of his passages I follow him perfectly. In speaking of the time of day for fly-fishing in the spring he says:

" 'Carpe diem' is a good watchword when trout are in the humor." At least, I know a good pun when I see one.

Fascinating Crimes

2. The Wallack Disappearances

SHORTLY after the Civil War the residents of Wallack, Connecticut, were awakened by the barking of a dog belonging to James Lenn, a visiting farmer. The dog was an old one, so they thought nothing of it, and went back to sleep again.

Later it was discovered that James Lenn was missing, and that the dog also had disappeared, but in the opposite direction. A search of the countryside was instituted which resulted in the finding of twenty-five empty tins, several old brooms, enough newspapers to make a fair-sized bale, and one old buggy-top. None of these seemed to have any value as clews in the mysterious disappearance of James Lenn. Some importance was attached to the discovery of the buggy-top until it was found that the missing farmer was not hiding under it.

The police, however, were not satisfied. There had been several violations of the State Fishing and Gaming ordinances in and around Wallack and public censure of the police was at its height. Chief of Police Walter M. Turbot determined to carry this case through to a finish. Thus it was that the search for Farmer James Lenn was begun afresh, a search which was destined to end in Innsbruck, Austria.

In the little town of Innsbruck there had been living an old garbler named Leon Nabgratz, a sort of town character, if such a thing were possible. Nabgratz had never been to America, but his young nephew, Gurling Nabgratz, son of Leon's brother

The principals in the famous Wallack disappearances
—Courtesy of John Held, Jr., and Life.

Meff, was born in that country and had lived there all his life. Late in December, 1867, he had moved to Wallack, Connecticut, where he was sold as a slave to one James Lenn.

One day, while reading the newspaper, Gurling Nabgratz came across an item indicating that slavery had been abolished four years previously and figured out that he was just a sap to be working for James Lenn for nothing. He mentioned the matter to his master, but Lenn maintained that it was only the Negro slaves who had been freed, and that Lincoln was no longer President anyway.

Nabgratz went away grumbling but did his chores that day as usual. He was seen late in the evening of April 17 in the poolroom of the village, where he is said to have made *sotto-voce* remarks and sung several slave songs of the ante-bellum South with such inflammatory refrains as "We'se all gwine ter be free!"

That night Gurling Nabgratz disappeared and was never seen again in Wallack.

This having preceded the disappearance of James Lenn by about two years, nothing was thought of it at the time. During the search for Lenn, however, the incident was recalled, and a search for Nabgratz was instituted. This made two searches going on at once in the little town of Wallack, and resulted in considerable hard feeling between the rival searching-parties. The town was divided into two camps, the "Find Lenn" faction and the "Find Nabgratz" faction, and on at least one occasion shots were exchanged.

In the meantime, in Innsbruck, Austria, Leon Nabgratz, the old garbler, was quietly pursuing his way, quite unconscious of the stir that he was causing four thousand miles away. His brother Meff had written him about Gurling's disappearance, but, as the old man never bothered to read his brother's letters, he was just as much in the dark as he had been before. More so, in fact, because he was older.

His surprise can well be imagined, therefore, when one day in the spring of 1869 the police entered his house in the Schmalzgasse and began a search for James Lenn of Wallack, Connecticut, U. S. A. In vain Nabgratz protested that he had never heard the name of Lenn and that, even if he had, it was not interesting to him. The arm of the law reaching across the Atlantic was inexorable. Leon Nabgratz's house was searched and in it was found an old trunk of suspiciously large proportions. In spite of the fact that this trunk was labeled *"Weihnachtsgeschenke"* ("Christmas presents") it was opened, and in it were found James Lenn *and* Gurling Nabgratz, together with a copy of the New York *Times* of October 12, 1868.

The mysterious Wallack disappearances were thus explained, and Leon Nabgratz was arrested for having in his possession a trunk with a misleading label on it.

Art is long and time is fleeting.

Kiddie-Kar
Travel

IN AMERICA there are two classes of travel—first class, and with children. Traveling with children corresponds roughly to traveling third-class in Bulgaria. They tell me there is nothing lower in the world than third-class Bulgarian travel.

The actual physical discomfort of traveling with the Kiddies is not so great, although you do emerge from it looking as if you had just moved the piano upstairs single-handed. It is the mental wear-and-tear that tells and for a sensitive man there is only one thing worse, and that is a church wedding in which he is playing the leading comedy rôle.

There are several branches of the ordeal of Going on Choo-Choo, and it is difficult to tell which is the roughest. Those who have taken a very small baby on a train maintain that this ranks as pleasure along with having a nerve killed. On the other hand, those whose wee companions are in the romping stage, simply laugh at the claims of the first group. Sometimes you will find a man who has both an infant *and* a romper with him. Such a citizen should receive a salute of twenty-one guns every time he enters the city and should be allowed to wear the insignia of the Pater Dolorosa, giving him the right to solicit alms on the cathedral steps.

97

There is much to be said for those who maintain that rather should the race be allowed to die out than that babies should be taken from place to place along our national arteries of traffic. On the other hand, there *are* moments when babies are asleep. (Oh, yes, there are. There *must* be.) But it is practically a straight run of ten or a dozen hours for your child of four. You may have a little trouble in getting the infant to doze off, especially as the train newsboy waits crouching in the vestibule until he sees signs of slumber on the child's face and then rushes in to yell, "Cop of *Life*, out today!" right by its pink, shell-like ear. But after it *is* asleep, your troubles are over except for wondering how you can shift your ossifying arm to a new position without disturbing its precious burden.

If the child is of an age which denies the existence of sleep, however, preferring to run up and down the aisle of the car rather than sit in its chair (at least a baby can't get out of its chair unless it falls out and even then it can't go far), then every minute of the trip is full of fun. On the whole, having traveled with children of all the popular ages, I would be inclined to award the Hair-Shirt to the man who successfully completes the ride with a boy of, let us say, three.

In the first place, you start with the pronounced ill-will of two-thirds of the rest of the occupants of the car. You see them as they come in, before the train starts, glancing at you and yours with little or no attempt to conceal the fact that they wish

You start with the pronounced ill-will of the rest of the occupants

they had waited for the four o'clock. Across from you is perhaps a large man who, in his home town, has a reputation for eating little children. He wears a heavy gold watch chain and wants to read through a lot of reports on the trip. He is just about as glad to be opposite a small boy as he would be if it were a hurdy-gurdy.

In back of you is a lady in a black silk dress who doesn't like the porter. Ladies in black silk dresses always seem to board the train with an aversion to the porter. The fact that the porter has to be in the same car with her makes her fussy to start with, and when she discovers that in front of her is a child of three who is already eating (you simply have to give him a lemon-drop to keep him quiet at least until the train starts), she decides that the best thing to do is simply to ignore him and not give him the slightest encouragement to become friendly. The child therefore picks her out immediately to be his buddy.

For a time after things get to going all you have to do is answer questions about the scenery. This is only what you must expect when you have children, and it happens no matter where you are. You can always say that you don't know who lives in that house or what that cow is doing. Sometimes you don't even have to look up when you say that you don't know. This part is comparatively easy.

It is when the migratory fit comes on that you will be put to the test. Suddenly you look and find the boy staggering down the aisle, peering into the faces of people as he passes them. "Here! Come back here, Roger!" you cry, lurching after him and landing across the knees of the young lady two seats down. Roger takes this as a signal for a game and starts to run, screaming with laughter. After four steps he falls and starts to cry.

On being carried kicking back to his seat, he is told that he mustn't run down the aisle again. This strikes even Roger as funny, because it is such a flat thing to say. Of course he is going to run down the aisle again and he knows it as well as you do.

In the meantime, however, he is perfectly willing to spend a little time with the lady in the black silk dress.

"Here, Roger," you say, "don't bother the lady."

"Hello, little boy," the lady says, nervously, and tries to go back to her book. The interview is over as far as she is concerned. Roger, however, thinks that it would be just dandy to get up in her lap. This has to be stopped, and Roger has to be whispered to.

He then announces that it is about time that he went to the wash-room. You march down the car, steering him by the shoulders and both lurching together as the train takes the curves and attracting wide attention to your very obvious excursion. Several kindly people smile knowingly at you as you pass and try to pat the boy on the head, but their advances are repelled, it being a rule of all children to look with disfavor on any attentions from strangers. The only people they want to play with are those who hate children.

On reaching the wash-room you discover that the porter has just locked it and taken the key with him, simply to be nasty. This raises quite a problem. You explain the situation as well as possible, which turns out to be not well enough. There is every indication of loud crying and perhaps worse. You call attention to the Burrows Rustless Screen sign which you are just passing and stand in the passage-way by the drinking-cups, feverishly trying to find things in the landscape as it whirls by which will serve to take the mind off the tragedy of the moment. You become so engrossed in this important task that it is some time before you discover that you are completely blocking the passage-way

Before you discover that you are completely blocking the passageway

and the progress of some fifteen people who want to get off at Utica. There is nothing for you to do but head the procession and get off first.

Once out in the open, the pride and prop of your old age decides that the thing to do is pay the engineer a visit, and starts off up the platform at a terrific rate. This amuses the onlookers and gives you a little exercise after being cramped up in that old car all the morning. The imminent danger of the train's starting without you only adds to the fun. At that, there might be worse things than being left in Utica. One of them is getting back on the train again to face the old gentleman with the large watch chain.

The final phase of the ordeal, however, is still in store for you when you make your way (and Roger's way) into the diner. Here the plunging march down the aisle of the car is multiplied by six (the diner is never any nearer than six cars and usually is part of another train). On the way, Roger sees a box of animal crackers belonging to a little girl and commandeers it. The little girl, putting up a fight, is promptly pushed over, starting what promises to be a free-for-all fight between the two families. Lurching along after the apologies have been made, it is just a series of unwarranted attacks by Roger on sleeping travelers and equally unwarranted evasions by Roger of the kindly advances of very nice people who love children.

In the diner, it turns out that the nearest thing they have suited to Roger's customary diet is veal cutlets, and you hardly think that his mother would approve of those. Everything else has peppers or sardines in it. A curry of lamb across the way strikes the boy's fancy and he demands some of that. On being told that he has not the slightest chance in the world of getting it but how would he like a little crackers-and-milk, he becomes quite upset and threatens to throw a fork at the Episcopal clergyman sitting opposite. Pieces of toast are waved alluringly in front of him and he is asked to consider the advantages of preserved figs and cream, but it is curry of lamb or he gets off the train. He doesn't act like this at home. In fact, he is noted for his tractability. There seems to be something about the train that brings out all the worst that is in him, all the hidden traits that he has inherited from his mother's side of the family. There is nothing else to do but say firmly: "Very well, then, Roger. We'll go back *without* any nice dinner," and carry him protesting from the diner, apologizing to the head steward for the scene and considering dropping him overboard as you pass through each vestibule.

In fact, I had a cousin once who had to take three of his little ones on an all-day trip from Philadelphia to Boston. It was the hottest day of the year and my cousin had on a woolen suit. By the time he reached Hartford, people in the car noticed that he had only two children with him. At Worcester he had only one. No one knew what had become of the others and no one asked. It seemed better not to ask. He reached Boston alone and never explained what had become of the tiny tots. Anyone who has ever traveled with tiny tots of his own, however, can guess.

The
Last Day

WHEN, during the long winter evenings, you
sit around the snap-shot album and recall
the merry, merry times you had on your vacation,
there is one day which your memory mercifully
overlooks. It is the day you packed up and left the
summer resort to go home.

This Ultimate Day really begins the night before,
when you sit up until one o'clock trying to get
things into the trunks and bags. This is when you
discover the well-known fact that summer air swells
articles to twice or three times their original size;
so that the sneakers which in June fitted in between
the phonograph and the book (which you have
never opened), in September are found to require
a whole tray for themselves and even then one of
them will probably have to be carried in the hand.

Along about midnight, the discouraging process
begins to get on your nerves and you snap at your
wife and she snaps at you every time it is found
that something won't fit in the suitcase. As you
have both gradually dispensed with the more attractive articles of clothing under stress of the heat and
the excitement, these little word passages taken on
the sordid nature of a squabble in an East Side
tenement, and all that is needed is for one of the

children to wake up and start whimpering. This it does.

It is finally decided that there is no sense in trying to finish the job that night. General nervousness, combined with a specific fear of oversleeping, results in a troubled tossing of perhaps three hours in bed, and ushers in the dawn of the last day on just about as irritable and bleary-eyed a little family as you will find outside an institution.

The trouble starts right away with the process of getting dressed in traveling clothes which haven't been worn since the trip up. Junior's shoulders are still tender, and he decides that it will be impossible for him to wear his starched blouse. One of Philip's good shoes, finding that there has been no call for it during the summer, has become hurt and has disappeared; so Philip has to wear a pair of Daddy's old bathing shoes which had been thrown away. (After everything has been locked and taken out of the room, the good shoe is found in the closet and left for dead.)

You, yourself, aren't any too successful in reverting to city clothes. Several weeks of soft collars and rubber-soled shoes have softened you to a point where the old "Deroy-14½" feels like a napkin-ring around your neck, and your natty brogans are so heavy that you lose your balance and topple over forward if you step out suddenly. The whole effect of your civilian costume when surveyed in a mirror is that of a Maine guide all dressed up for an outing "up to Bangor."

Incidentally, it shapes up as one of the hottest days of the season—or any other season.

"Oh, look how funny Daddy looks in his straw hat!"

"I never realized before, Fred, how much too high the crown is for the length of your face. Are you sure it's your hat?"

"It's my hat, all right," is the proper reply, "but maybe the face belongs to somebody else."

This silences them for a while, but on and off during the day a lot of good-natured fun is had in calling the attention of outsiders to the spectacle presented by Daddy in his "store" clothes.

Once everyone is dressed, there must be an excursion to take one last look at the ocean, or lake, or whatever particular prank of Nature it may have been which has served as an inducement to you to leave the city. This must be done before breakfast. So down to the beach you go, getting your shoes full of sand, and wait while Sister, in a sentimental attempt to feel the water for the last time, has tripped and fallen in, soaking herself to the garters. There being no dry clothes left out, she has to go in the kitchen and stand in front of the stove until at least one side of her is dry.

Breakfast bears no resemblance to any other meal eaten in the place. There is a poorly-suppressed feeling that you must hurry, coupled with the stiff collar and tight clothes, which makes it practically impossible to get any food down past the upper chest.

Then follows one of the worst features of the worst of all vacation days—the goodbyes. It isn't that you hate to part company with these people. They too, as they stand there in their summer clothes, seem to have undergone some process whereby you see them as they really are and not as they seemed when you were all together up to your necks in water or worrying a tennis ball back and forth over a net. And you may be sure that you, in your town clothes, seem doubly unattractive to them.

Here is Mrs. Tremble, who lives in Montclair, N. J., in the winter. That really is a terrible hat of hers, now that you get a good look at it. "Well, goodbye, Mrs. Tremble. Be sure to look us up if you ever get out our way. We are right in the telephone book, and we'll have a regular get-together meeting. . . . Goodbye, Marian. Think of us tonight in the hot city, and be sure to let us know when you are going through . . . Well, so long, Mr. Prothero; look out for those girls up at the post office. Don't let any of them marry you . . . Well, we're off, Mrs. Rostetter. Yes, we're leaving today. On the 10-45. We have to be back for Junior's school. It begins on the 11th. *Good*bye!"

It is then found that there is about an hour to wait before the machine comes to take you to the station; so all these goodbyes have been wasted and have to be gone through with again.

In the meantime, Mother decides that she must run over to the Bide-a-Wee cottage and say goodbye

Sister has tripped and fallen in, soaking herself to the garters

to the Sisbys. The children feel that they are about due for another last look at the ocean. And Daddy remembers that he hasn't been able to shut the big suitcase yet. So the family disperses in various directions and each unit gets lost. Mother, rushing out from the Sisbys' in a panic thinking that she hears the automobile, is unable to find the others. Little Mildred, having taken it upon herself to look out for the other children while they are gazing on the ocean, has felt it incumbent on her to spank Philip for trying to build one last tunnel in the sand, resulting in a bitter physical encounter in which Philip easily batters his sister into a state of hysteria. Daddy, having wilted his collar and put his knee through his straw hat in an attempt to jam the suitcase together, finds that the thing can't be done and takes out the box of sea-shells that Junior had planned to take home for his cabinet, and hides them under the bed.

The suitcase at last having been squeezed shut and placed with the rest of the bags in the hall, the maid comes running up with five damp bathing suits which she has found hanging on the line and wants to know if they belong here. Daddy looks cautiously down the hall and whispers: "No!"

At last the automobile arrives and stands honking by the roadside. "Come, Junior, quick, put your coat on! . . . Have you got the bag with the thermos? . . . Hurry, Philip! . . . Where's Sister? . . . Come, Sister! . . . Well, it's too late now. You'll have to wait till we get on the train . . .

Looks cautiously down the hall and whispers: "No!"

Goodbye, Mrs. Tremble . . . Be sure to look us up . . . Goodbye, everybody! . . . Here, Junior! Put that down! You can't take that with you. No, no! That belongs to that other little boy . . . *Junior!* . . . Goodbye, Marian! . . . Goodbye, Mrs. McNerdle! . . . Philip, say goodbye to Mrs. McNerdle, she's been so good to you, don't you remember? . . . Goodbye, Mrs. McNerdle, that's right. . . . *Goodbye!*"

And with that the automobile starts, the friends

on the porch wave and call out indistinguishable pleasantries, Junior begins to cry, and it is found that Ed has no hat.

The trip home in the heat and cinders is enlivened by longing reminiscences: "Well, it's eleven o'clock. I suppose they're all getting into their bathing suits now. How'd you like to jump into that old ocean right this minute, eh?" (As a matter of fact, the speaker has probably not been induced to go into "that old ocean" more than three times during the whole summer.)

The fact that they reach home too late to get a regular dinner and have to go to bed hungry, and the more poignant impressions in the process of opening a house which has been closed all summer, have all been treated of before in an article called "The Entrance Into the Tomb." And so we will leave our buoyant little family, their vacation ended, all ready to jump into the swing of their work, refreshed, invigorated, and clear-eyed.

Family Life in America

PART 1

The naturalistic literature of this country has reached such a state that no family of characters is considered true to life which does not include at least two hypochondriacs, one sadist, and one old man who spills food down the front of his vest. If this school progresses, the following is what we may expect in our national literature in a year or so.

THE living-room in the Twillys' house was so damp that thick, soppy moss grew all over the walls. It dripped on the picture of Grandfather Twilly that hung over the melodeon, making streaks down the dirty glass like sweat on the old man's face. It was a mean face. Grandfather Twilly had been a mean man and had little spots of soup on the lapel of his coat. All his children were mean and had soup spots on their clothes.

Grandma Twilly sat in the rocker over by the window, and as she rocked the chair snapped. It sounded like Grandma Twilly's knees snapping as they did whenever she stooped over to pull the wings off a fly. She was a mean old thing. Her knuckles were grimy and she chewed crumbs that she found in the bottom of her reticule. You would have hated her. She hated herself. But most of all she hated Grandfather Twilly.

114

"I certainly hope you're frying good," she muttered as she looked up at his picture.

"Hasn't the undertaker come yet, Ma?" asked young Mrs. Wilbur Twilly petulantly. She was boiling water on the oil-heater and every now and again would spill a little of the steaming liquid on the baby who was playing on the floor. She hated the baby because it looked like her father. The hot water raised little white blisters on the baby's red neck and Mabel Twilly felt short, sharp twinges of pleasure at the sight. It was the only pleasure she had had for four months.

"Why don't you kill yourself, Ma?" she continued. "You're only in the way here and you know it. It's just because you're a mean old woman and want to make trouble for us that you hang on."

Grandma Twilly shot a dirty look at her daughter-in-law. She had always hated her. Stringy hair, Mabel had. Dank, stringy hair. Grandma Twilly thought how it would look hanging at an Indian's belt. But all that she did was to place her tongue against her two front teeth and make a noise like the bath-room faucet.

Wilbur Twilly was reading the paper by the oil lamp. Wilbur had watery blue eyes and cigar ashes all over his knees. The third and fourth buttons of his vest were undone. It was too hideous.

He was conscious of his family seated in chairs about him. His mother, chewing crumbs. His wife Mabel, with her stringy hair, reading. His sister Bernice, with projecting front teeth, who sat thinking of the man who came every day to take away the waste paper. Bernice was wondering how long it would be before her family would discover that she had been married to this man for three years.

How Wilbur hated them all. It didn't seem as if he could stand it any longer. He wanted to scream and stick pins into every one of them and then rush out and see the girl who worked in his office snapping rubber-bands all day. He hated her too, but she wore side-combs.

PART 2

The street was covered with slimy mud. It oozed out from under Bernice's rubbers in unpleasant bubbles until it seemed to her as if she must kill herself. Hot air coming out from a steam laundry. Hot, stifling air. Bernice didn't work in the laundry but she wished that she did so that the hot air would kill her. She wanted to be stifled. She needed torture to be happy. She also needed a good swift clout on the side of the face.

A drunken man lurched out from a door-way and flung his arms about her. It was only her husband. She loved her husband. She loved him so much that, as she pushed him away and into the gutter, she stuck her little finger into his eye. She also untied his neck-tie. It was a bow neck-tie, with white, dirty spots on it and it was wet with gin. It didn't seem as if Bernice could stand it any longer. All the repressions of nineteen sordid years behind protruding teeth surged through her untidy soul.

She wanted love. But it was not her husband that she loved so fiercely. It was old Grandfather Twilly. And he was too dead.

PART 3

In the dining-room of the Twilly's house everything was very quiet. Even the vinegar-cruet which was covered with fly-specks. Grandma Twilly lay with her head in the baked potatoes, poisoned by Mabel, who, in her turn had been poisoned by her husband and sprawled in an odd posture over the china-closet. Wilbur and his sister Bernice had just finished choking each other to death and between them completely covered the carpet in that corner of the room where the worn spot showed the bare boards beneath, like ribs on a chicken carcass.

Only the baby survived. She had a mean face and had great spillings of Imperial Granum down her bib. As she looked about her at her family, a great hate surged through her tiny body and her eyes snapped viciously. She wanted to get down from her high-chair and show them all how much she hated them.

Bernice's husband, the man who came after the waste paper, staggered into the room. The tips were off both his shoe-lacings. The baby experienced a voluptuous sense of futility at the sight of the tipless-lacings and leered suggestively at her uncle-in-law.

"We must get the roof fixed," said the man, very quietly. "It lets the sun in."

The Romance of Digestion

WHEN you take a bite of that delicious cookie, or swallow a morsel of that nourishing bread, do you stop to think of the marvelous and intricate process by means of which Mother Nature is going to convert it into bone and sinew and roses for those pretty cheeks? Probably not, and it is just as well. For if you did stop to think of it at that time, you would unquestionably not be able to digest that cookie—or that nourishing bread.

But whether you think of it or not this exciting process of digestion is going on, day in and day out, sometimes pretty badly but always with a great show of efficiency. It is, on the whole, probably one of the worst-done jobs in the world.

First you must know that those hard, white edges of bone which you must have noticed hundreds of times along the front of your mouth, are "teeth," and are put there for a very definite purpose. They are the ivory gates to the body. They are Nature's tiny sentinels, and if you have ever bitten yourself, you will know how sharp they can be, and what efficient little watchmen they are. Just you try to slip your finger into your mouth without your teeth's permission, and see how far you get. Or try to get it out, once they have captured it.

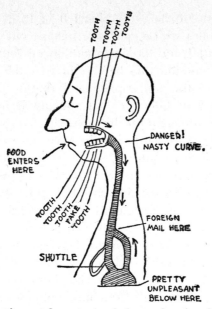

Labels in image: TOOTH TOOTH TOOTH TOOTH, DANGER! NASTY CURVE., FOOD ENTERS HERE, TOOTH TOOTH TOOTH FAKE TOOTH, FOREIGN MAIL HERE, SHUTTLE, PRETTY UNPLEASANT BELOW HERE

Cross section of human food duct, showing ludicrous process of self-styled "Digestion"

Now these thousands of brave little soldiers, the teeth, which we have in our mouths, take the food as it comes through the air (in case you are snapping at a butterfly) or from the fork, and separate it into its component parts (air, land and water). In this process, the teeth are aided by the tongue, which is that awful-looking thing right back of your teeth. Don't look at it!

The tongue (which we may call the escalator of the mouth or Nature's nobleman for short), and the teeth toss the food back and forth between

119

them until there is nothing left of it, except the little bones which you have to take out between your thumb and forefinger and lay on your butter-plate. In doing this be careful that the bone is really on the butter-plate and that it does not stick to your finger so that you put it back into your mouth again on the next trip, for this would make the little white sentries very angry and they might all drop out.

And now comes the really wonderful part of the romance which is being enacted right there under your very eyes. A chemical reaction on the tongue presses a little button which telegraphs down, down, down, 'way down to the cross old Stomach and says: "Please, sir, do you want this food or don't you?" And the Stomach, whom we shall call "Prince Charming" from now on, telegraphs (or more likely writes) back: "Yes, dear!" or "You can do what you like with it for all of me." Just as he happens to feel at the time.

And then, such a hurry and bustle as goes on in the mouth! "Foodie's going to visit Stomach!" all the little teeth cry, and rush about for all the world as if they were going themselves. "All aboard, all aboard!" calls out the tongue, and there is a great ringing of bells and blowing of whistles and bumping of porters and in the midst of it all, the remnants of that delicious cookie seated nervously on the tongue, ready to be taken down on its first journey alone, down to see Prince Charming. For all the joyousness of the occasion, it is a little sad, too. For that bit of cookie is going to get some terribly tough treatment before it is through.

The food is then placed on a conveyor, by means of which it is taken to the Drying Room, situated on the third floor, where it is taken apart and washed and dried, preparatory to going through the pressing machines. These pressing machines are operated by one man, who stands by the conveyor as it brings the food along and tosses it into the vats. Here all rocks and moss are drawn off by mechanical pickers and the food subjected to treatment in a solution of sulphite, a secret process which is jealously guarded. From here the food is taken to the Playroom where it plays around awhile with the other children until it is time for it to be folded by the girls in the bindery, packed into neat stacks, and wrapped for shipment in bundles of fifty. Some of these bundles, the proteins, are shipped to the bones of the body, others, the hydrates, go to making muscle, while a third class, the sophomores, contribute to making fatty tissue which nobody wants, that is, not if he has any pride at all about his appearance. The by-products are made into milk-bottle caps, emery wheels, and insurance calendars, and are sold at cost.

Thus we see how wonderfully Nature takes care of us and our little troubles, aided only by soda-mint and bicarbonate.

"Ask that Man"

THIS is written for those men who have wives who are constantly insisting on their asking questions of officials.

For years I was troubled with the following complaint: Just as soon as we started out on a trip of any kind, even if it were only to the corner of the street, Doris began forcing me to ask questions of people. If we weren't quite sure of the way: "Why don't you ask that man? He could tell you." If there was any doubt as to the best place to go to get chocolate ice-cream, she would say: "Why don't you ask that boy in uniform? He would be likely to know."

I can't quite define my aversion to asking questions of strangers. From snatches of family battles which I have heard drifting up from railway stations and street corners, I gather that there are a great many men who share my dislike for it, as well as an equal number of women who, like Doris, believe it to be the solution of most of this world's problems. The man's dread is probably that of making himself appear a pest or ridiculously uninformed. The woman's insistence is based probably on experience which has taught her that *any* one, no matter who, knows more about things in general than her husband.

Furthermore, I never know exactly how to begin

122

I gather that there are a great many men who share my dislike for it

a request for information. If I preface it with, "I beg your pardon!" the stranger is likely not to hear, especially if he happens to be facing in another direction, for my voice isn't very reliable in

My voice isn't very reliable in crises

crises and sometimes makes no intelligible sound at all until I have been talking for fully a minute. Often I say, "I beg your pardon!" and he turns quickly and says, "What did you say?" Then I have to repeat, "I beg your pardon!" and he asks, quite naturally, "What for?" Then I am stuck. Here I am, begging a perfect stranger's pardon, and for no apparent reason under the sun. The wonder is that I am not knocked down oftener.

It was to avoid going through life under this pressure that I evolved the little scheme detailed herewith. It cost me several thousand dollars, but Doris is through with asking questions of outsiders.

We had started on a little trip to Boston. I could have found out where the Boston train was in a few minutes had I been left to myself. But Doris never relies on the signs. Someone must be asked, too, just to make sure. Confronted once by a buckboard literally swathed in banners which screamed in red letters, "This bus goes to the State Fair Grounds," I had to go up to the driver (who had on his cap a flag reading "To the State Fair Grounds") and ask him if this bus surely went to the State Fair Grounds. He didn't even answer me.

So when Doris said: "Go and ask that man where the Boston train leaves from," I gritted my teeth and decided that the time had come. Simulating conversation with him, I really asked him nothing, and returned to Doris, saying, "Come on. He says it goes from Track 10."

Eight months later we returned home. The train that left on Track 10 was the Chicago Limited, which I had taken deliberately. In Chicago I again falsified what "the man" told me, and instead of getting on the train back to New York we went to Little Rock, Arkansas. Every time I had to ask where the best hotel was, I made up information which brought us out into the suburbs, cold and hungry. Many nights we spent wandering through the fields looking for some place that never existed, or else in the worst hotel in town acting on what I said was the advice of "that kind-looking man in uniform."

From Arkansas, we went into Mexico, and once, guided by what I told her had been the directions given me by the man at the news-stand in Vera Cruz, we made a sally into the swamps of Central America, in whatever that first republic is on the way south. After that, Doris began to lose faith in what strange men could tell us. One day, at a little station in Mavicos, I said: "Wait a minute, till I ask that man what is the best way to get back into America," and she said, sobbing: "Don't ask anybody. Just do what you think is best." Then I knew that the fight was over. In ten days I had her limp form back in New York and from that day to this she hasn't once suggested that I ask questions of a stranger.

The funny part of it is, I constantly find myself asking them. I guess the humiliation came in being told to ask.

Cell-formations and
Their Work

IT IS only recently that science has found out the exact structure of the tiny cell-formations which go to make up life. Only yesterday, in fact.

Every higher animal starts life as a single cell. This much is obvious. Look at the rainbow. Look at the formation of frost on the window-pane. Don't look now. Wait a minute. . . . Now look.

This cell measures no more than 1/125 of an inch in diameter at first, but you mustn't be discouraged. It looks like nothing at all, even under the strongest microscope, and, before we knew just how important they were, they were often thrown away. We now know that if it were not for these tiny, tiny cells, we should none of us be here today. This may or may not be a recommendation for the cells. *Quien sabe?*

Shortly after the cell decides to go ahead with the thing, it gets lonely and divides itself up into three similar cells, just for company's sake and to have someone to talk to. They soon find out that they aren't particularly congenial, so they keep on dividing themselves up into other cells until there is a regular mob of them. Then they elect an entertainment committee and give a show.

After the show, there is a fight, and the thing

breaks up into different cliques or groups. One group think they are white corpuscles or *phagocytes*. Others go around saying that they are *red* corpuscles and to hell with the white.

The other groups of cells devote themselves to music, æsthetic dancing, and the formation of starch which goes into dress-shirts. They are all very happy and very busy, and it's nobody's business *what* they do when they aren't working. We certainly are not going to snoop into that here.

We must take up, however, the work of the brain-cells, as it is in the brain that the average man of today does his thinking. (Aha-ha-ha-ha-ha-ha!)

Oh, let's *not* take up the brain-cells. You know as much about them as anybody does, and what's the use anyway? Suppose you *do* learn something today. You're likely to die tomorrow, and there you are.

And we *must* go into the question of the size of these cells. That really is important. In about 1/150000 of a cubic inch of blood there are some five million cells afloat. This is, as you will see, about the population of the City of London, except that the cells don't wear any hats. Thus, in our whole body, there are perhaps (six times seven is forty-two, five times eight is forty, put down naught and carry your four, eight times nine is seventy-two and four is seventy-six, put down six and carry your seven and then, adding, six, four, three, one, six, naught, naught, naught), oh, about a billion or so of these red corpuscles alone, not counting over-head and breakage. In the course of time, that runs into figures.

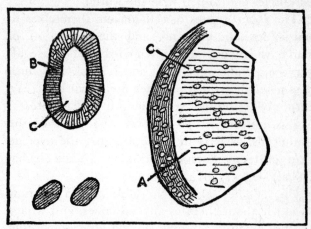

Differentiation of cells in the lens of an eye. Doesn't mean a thing

Now when it comes to reproduction, you have to look out. In the cuttlefish, for example, there is what is known as "greesion" or budding. The organism as a whole remains unaltered, except that one small portion of it breaks off and goes into business for itself. This, of course, makes a very pretty picture, but gets nowhere. In the case of multicellular animals, like the orange, it results in a frightful confusion.

We should have said that there are two classes of animals, unicellular and multicellular. From the unicellular group we get our coal, iron, wheat and ice, and from the multicellular our salt, pepper, chutney and that beautiful silk dress which milady wears so proudly. Woolen and leather goods we import.

You will see then that by grafting a piece of one species on another species, you can mix the cells and have all kinds of fun. Winkler, in 1902, grafted a piece of Solanum (the genus to which the potato belongs) onto a stock of another kind, and then, after the union had been established, cut the stem across, just at the point of junction. The bud was formed of the intermingled tissues of the two species and was most peculiar-looking.

Winkler was arrested.

Editha's
Christmas Burglar

I T WAS the night before Christmas, and Editha was all agog. It was all so exciting, so exciting! From her little bed up in the nursery she could hear Mumsey and Daddy down-stairs putting the things on the tree and jamming her stocking full of broken candy and oranges.

"Hush!" Daddy was speaking. "Eva," he was saying to Mumsey, "it seems kind of silly to put this ten-dollar gold-piece that Aunt Issac sent to Editha into her stocking. She is too young to know the value of money. It would just be a bauble to her. How about putting it in with the household money for this month? Editha would then get some of the food that was bought with it and we would be ten dollars in."

Dear old Daddy! Always thinking of someone else! Editha wanted to jump out of bed right then and there and run down and throw her arms about his neck, perhaps shutting off his wind.

"You are right, as usual, Hal," said Mumsey. "Give me the gold-piece and I will put it in with the house funds."

"In a pig's eye I will give you the gold-piece," replied Daddy. "You would nest it away some-where until after Christmas and then go out and

132

buy yourself a muff with it. I know you, you old grafter." And from the sound which followed, Editha knew that Mumsey was kissing Daddy. Did ever a little girl have two such darling parents? And, hugging her Teddy-bear close to her, Editha rolled over and went to sleep.

.   .   .   .   .

She awoke suddenly with the feeling that someone was downstairs. It was quite dark and the radiolite traveling-clock which stood by her bedside said eight o'clock, but, as the radiolite traveling-clock hadn't been running since Easter, she knew that that couldn't be the right time. She knew that it must be somewhere between three and four in the morning, however, because the blanket had slipped off her bed, and the blanket always slipped off her bed between three and four in the morning.

And now to take up the question of who it was downstairs. At first she thought it might be Daddy. Often Daddy sat up very late working on a case of Scotch and at such times she would hear him downstairs counting to himself. But whoever was there now was being very quiet. It was only when he jammed against the china-cabinet or joggled the dinner-gong that she could tell that anyone was there at all. It was evidently a stranger.

Of course, it might be that the old folks had been right all along and that there really was a Santa Claus after all, but Editha dismissed this supposition at once. The old folks had never been right before and what chance was there of their starting in to be right now, at their age? None at all. It couldn't be Santa, the jolly old soul!

It must be a burglar then! Why, to be sure! Burglars always come around on Christmas Eve and little yellow-haired girls always get up and go down in their nighties and convert them. Of course! How silly of Editha not to have thought of it before!

With a bound the child was out on the cold floor, and with another bound she was back in bed again. It was too cold to be fooling around without slippers on. Reaching down by the bedside, she pulled in her little fur foot-pieces which Cousin Mabel had left behind by mistake the last time she visited Editha, and drew them on her tiny feet. Then out she got and started on tip-toe for the stairway.

She did hope that he would be a good-looking burglar and easily converted, because it was pretty gosh-darned cold, even with slippers on, and she wished to save time.

As she reached the head of the stairs, she could look down into the living-room where the shadow of the tree stood out black against the gray light outside. In the doorway leading into the dining room stood a man's figure, silhouetted against the glare of an old-fashioned burglar's lantern which was on the floor. He was rattling silverware. Very quietly, Editha descended the stairs until she stood quite close to him.

"Hello, Mr. Man!" she said.

"Hello, Mr. Man!" she said

The burglar looked up quickly and reached for his gun.

"Who the hell do you think you are?" he asked.

"I'se Editha," replied the little girl in the sweetest voice she could summon, which wasn't particularly sweet at that as Editha hadn't a very pretty voice.

"You's Editha, is youse?" replied the burglar. "Well, come on down here. Grandpa wants to speak to you."

"Youse is not my Drandpa," said the tot getting her baby and tough talk slightly mixed. "Youse is a dreat, bid burglar."

"All right, kiddy," replied the man. "Have it your own way. But come on down. I want ter show yer how yer kin make smoke come outer yer eyes. It's a Christmas game."

"This guy is as good as converted already," thought Editha to herself. "Right away he starts wanting to teach me games. Next he'll be telling me I remind him of his little girl at home."

So with a light heart she came the rest of the way downstairs, and stood facing the burly stranger.

"Sit down, Editha," he said, and gave her a hearty push which sent her down heavily on the floor. "And stay there, or I'll mash you one on that baby nose of yours."

This was not in the schedule as Editha had read it in the books, but it doubtless was this particular burglar's way of having a little fun. He *did* have nice eyes, too.

"Dat's naughty to do," she said, scoldingly.

"Yeah?" said the burglar, and sent her spinning against the wall. "I guess you need attention, kid. You can't be trusted." Whereupon he slapped the little girl. Then he took a piece of rope out of his bag and tied her up good and tight, with a nice bright bandana handkerchief around her mouth, and trussed her up on the chandelier.

"Now hang there," he said, "and make believe you're a Christmas present, and if you open yer yap, I'll set fire to yer."

Then, filling his bag with the silverware and Daddy's imitation sherry, Editha's burglar tip-toed out by the door. As he left, he turned and smiled. "A Merry Christmas to all and to all a Good Night," he whispered, and was gone.

"A Merry Christmas to all and to all a Good Night!"

And when Mumsey and Daddy came down in the morning, there was Editha up on the chandelier, sore as a crab. So they took her down and spanked her for getting out of bed without permission.

137

A Short History of
American Politics

THOSE of you who get around to reading a lot will remember that a history of American politics was begun by me several chapters back— or rather, an introduction to such a history was written. Then came the Great War . . . brother was turned against brother, father against father; the cobblestones of the Tuileries were spattered with the blood of the royalists, and such minor matters as histories were cast aside for the musket and ploughshare. In crises such as that of March, 1928, the savants must give way to the men of action.

Now that the tumult and the shouting have died, however, the history of American politics can be written. The only trouble at present is that I have lost the introduction I wrote several months ago. It must have fallen down behind the bureau and the wall of the Kremlin.

To write another introductory preface would be silly, and that is the reason I have decided to write one. The other one was probably not much good, anyway. So while you all go ahead and read the other pages of this volume, I will write another introduction to a history of American politics. (That is, I will if I can get this stuff off the keys

of my typewriter. Either somebody has rubbed
candy over each key while I have been dozing here
or the typewriter itself has a strain of maple in it
and is giving off sap. I have never run across anything like it in all my experience with typewriters.
The "j" key looks so sticky that I am actually afraid
to touch it. Ugh!)

Well, anyway ——

A HISTORY OF AMERICAN POLITICS

(2 vol., 695 pp. 8vo................100 to 1 to show.)

INTRODUCTION

The theory of political procedure in those coun-
tries in which a democratic form of government ob-
tains is based on the assumption that the average
citizen knows enough to vote. (*Time out for pro-
longed laughter.*)

The Ideal State of Plato, as you will remember
(you liar!), was founded on quite a different principle, but, if you will look at Greece today you
will see that something was wrong in that principle,
too. Plato felt—and quite rightly—that Truth is
the Ultimate Good and that the Ultimate Good is
Truth—or the Idea. (Check one of these three.)
Now—in the Ideal State, granted that the citizens
keep away from the polls and mind their own business, we have an oligarchy or combination of
hydrogen atoms so arranged as to form Truth in
the Abstract. Of course, Plato wrote only what he

139

had learned from Socrates, and Socrates, like the wise old owl that he was, never signed his name to anything. So that left Plato holding the bag for an unworkable political theory which has been carried down to the present day.

Aristotle followed Plato with some new theories, but as he dealt mostly with the Drama and Mathematics, with side excursions into Bird Raising and Exercises for the Eye, we don't have to bother with his ideas on Government. I don't remember what they were, in the first place.

This brings us up to 1785, when the United States began to have its first political prickly-heat. It may have been a little before 1785 (I am working entirely without notes or reference books in this history), but 1785 is near enough, for the Revolution didn't end until around 1782, or 1780, and that would leave a couple of years for George Washington to begin his two terms as President and get things good and balled up. So we will say 1785.

Here we are, then, a new country, faced with an experiment in government and working on nothing sounder than a belief that the average voter is entitled to have a hand in the running of the State. The wonder is that we have got as far as we have —or *have* we?

Now, in this introduction I have tried to outline the main influences in political thought which culminated in the foundation of our form of government. I have omitted any reference to Lebœuf and

Froissart, because, so far as I know, Lebœuf and Froissart never had any ideas on the subject; at any rate, not the Lebœuf that I knew. I have not gone into the Hanseatic League or the Guild System, not through any pique on my part, but because, after all, they involved a quite different approach to the question of democratic government and I couldn't find any pictures which would illustrate them interestingly. If, however, any of my readers are anxious to look up the Hanseatic League, I can refer them to a very good book on the subject called "The Hanseatic League."

The Lost
Language

AT THE meeting of the International Philol-
ogists' Association in Lucerne last April
(1923-1925), something in the nature of a bomb-
shell was thrown by Professor Eric Nunsen of the
University of Ulholm. Professor Nunsen, in a
paper entitled, "Aryan Languages: The Funny
Old Things," declared that in between the Hamitic group of languages and the Ural-Altaic group
there should by rights come another and hitherto
uncharted group, to be known as the Semi-Huinty
group. Professor Nunsen's paper followed a number on the program called "Al Holtz and His Six
Musical Skaters."

According to this eminent philologist, too much
attention has been paid in the past to root words.
By "root words" we mean those words which look
like roots of some kind or other when you draw
pictures of them. These words recur in similar
form in all the languages which comprise a certain group. Thus, in the Aryan group, compare, for
example, the English *dish-towel*, Gothic *dersh-terl*,
German *tish-döl*, Latin *dec-tola*, French *dis-toil*,
Armenian *dash-taller*, Sanskrit *dit-toll* and Dutch
dösh-tööller. In all of these words you will note the
same absurdity.

In the same manner it is easy to trace the similarity between languages of the same group by noting, as in the Semitic group, that the fundamental *f* in Arabic becomes *w* in Assyrian, and the capital *G* in Phœnician becomes a small *g* in Abyssinian. This makes it hard for Assyrian traveling salesmen, as they have no place to leave their grips.

In his interesting work, "The Mutations of the Syllable *Bib* Between 2000 and 500 B. C.," Landoc Downs traces the use of the letter *h* down through Western Asia with the Caucasian migration into Central Europe, and there loses it. For perhaps two thousand years we have no record of the letter *h* being used by Nordics. This is perhaps not strange, as the Nordics at that time didn't use much of anything. And then suddenly, in about 1200 B. C., the letter *h* shows up again in Northern Ohio, this time under the alias of *m* and clean-shaven. There is no question, however, but that it is the old Bantu *h* in disguise, and we are thus able to tell that the two peoples (the Swiss and that other one) are really of the same basic stock. Any one could tell that; so don't be silly.

Now, says Professor Nunsen, it is quite probable that this change in root words, effected by the passage of the Aryan-speaking peoples north of the Danube, Dneiper and Don (the "D" in Danube is silent, making the word pronounced "Anube"), so irritated the Hamitic group (which included ancient Egyptian, Coptic, Berber and Otto H. Kahn) that they began dropping the final *g* just out of spite. This, in the course of several centuries, re-

143

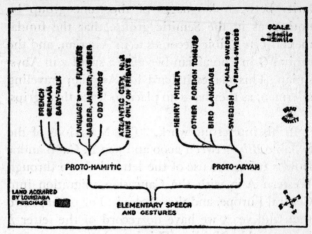

Chart showing relation of lost language (semi-Huinty)
to other Language groups and to itself

sulted in the formation of a quite distinct group, the one which Professor Nunsen calls the "Semi-Huinty." It is not *entirely* Huinty, for there still remain traces of the old Hamitic. Just *semi-*Huinty. Even *semi* is quite a lot.

This, of course, takes no notice of the Ural-Altaic group. That is quite all right. No one ever does. This group includes the Lappish, Samoyed, Magyar and Tartar, and, as Dr. Kneeland Renfrew says in his "Useless Languages: Their Origin and Excuse": "There is no sense in bothering with the Ural-Altaic group."

So Professor Nunsen has some authority for disregarding the question of grammatical gender, and it is on this point that he bases his discovery of the existence of the Semi-Huinty languages. These languages, he says, are monosyllabic and have no inflections, the tone used in uttering a word determining its meaning. In this it is similar to the Chinese tongue, which is one of the reasons why China is so far away from the European continent.

Thus the word *reezyl*, uttered in one tone, means "Here comes the postman" in another tone, "There is a button off this pair," and, in still a third tone, "you" (diminutive).

It will be seen from this how difficult it is for the philologist to do anything more than guess at just what the lost languages were really like. He is not sure that they are even lost. If they were *not* really lost, then the joke is on Professor Nunsen for having gone to all this trouble for nothing.

Museum
Feet

A Complaint Contracted by Over-zealous Parents

THERE is one big danger in the approach of Autumn, and that is that the snappy weather may excite us into making plans for doing things we ought to have done long ago. Those of us who are parents are likely to decide that we haven't been paying enough attention to the children, that we ought to take them out more to places of interest and instruction. More of a pal than a father, is what we feel we ought to be, and yet withal an instructor, steering them into enlightening byways and taking them on educational trips to fisheries and jute manufactories, etc.

Now this is just a manifestation of Fall Fever, and will die down, so don't give in to it. Let the children educate themselves. You haven't done such a swell job with yourself that you should undertake to show someone else how to do it. And, above all, never take the kiddies to a natural history museum. Taking them to a natural history museum is one of the things a parent first feels coming on when the crisp Autumn days send the blood tingling through his veins, and it's one of the last things he should do.

I, myself, in a burst of parental obligation last Fall, decided to take the boys through the Smithsonian Institution in Washington. I would have picked a *bigger* place if there had been one in the country, but the Smithsonian was the biggest I could get. As a result I contracted a bad case of what is known in medical circles as "Smithsonian feet," that is, a complete paralysis of the feet from the ankles down, due to standing on first one foot and then the other in front of exhibition cases and walking miles upon miles up and down the tessellated corridors of the museum. The boys suffered no ill effects from the trip at all.

The sad thing about a trip through a museum with the children is that you start out with so much vigor and zip. On entering the main entrance lobby, you call back Herbert who takes a running slide across the smooth floor, and tell him that he must stay close to Daddy and that Daddy will show him everything and explain everything. And what a sap that makes Daddy before the day is done!

In your care not to miss anything, you stop and examine carefully the very first tablet in the entrance lobby, deciding to work to the left and look at everything on the left side of the building, and then take up the right side.

"Look, boys," you say, "it says here that this building was built by the Natural History Society of America in 1876—Oh, well, I guess that isn't very important." And you ask the attendant at the door which is the most satisfactory way to see the museum, a foolish question at best. He tells you to begin with the Glacier Hall over there at the right. This upsets your plans a little, but what difference does it make whether you see the right or left side first?

"Come on, boys," you call to both of them who are now sliding back and forth on the floor. "Here is the room where the glaciers are. Come on and look at the glaciers."

The boys by this time are very hot and sweaty, and probably less interested in glaciers than in anything else in the world. You, yourself, find nothing particularly thrilling about the rocks which are lined up for inspection in the room as you enter. However, it is a pretty important thing, this matter of glacial deposits, and both you and the boys would be better off for knowing a little something about them.

"Look, Herbert," you say. "Look, Arthur! See here where the glacier went right over this rock and left these big marks."

But Herbert is already in the next hall, which for some mysterious reason is devoted to stuffed rats demonstrating the Malthusian Doctrine—and Arthur has disappeared entirely.

"Where's Arthur, Herbert?" you yell.

"Look, Daddy," replies Herbert from across the hall. "Come here quick! Quick, Daddy!" There evidently is some danger that the stuffed rats are going to get away before you arrive, and you have to run to hush Herbert up, although you had much

*Arthur has by this time appeared several miles down
the building*

rather not look at stuffed rats, Malthusian Doctrine
or no Malthusian Doctrine.

Arthur has, by this time, appeared several miles
down the building in the Early American Indian
Room and screams:

"Come quick, Daddy! Look! Indians!"

So you and Herbert set off on a dog trot to the
Early American Indian Room.

"You boys *must not* yell so in here," you warn.
"And stop running, Arthur! We've got all day
(God forbid!)."

"Where did these Indians live, Daddy?" asks
Herbert.

"Oh, around Massachusetts," you explain. "They
fought the Pilgrims."

"It says here they lived in Arizona," reads Arthur. (Whoever taught that boy to read, anyway?)

"Well, Arizona *too*," you crawl. "They lived all
over."

"What are these, Daddy?"

"Those? Those are hatchet-heads. They used
them for heads to their hatchets."

"It says here they are flint stones that they struck
fire on."

"Flint stones, eh? Well, they're funny-looking
flint stones. They must have used them for hatchet-
heads, too."

"What did they use these for, Daddy?"

"If you can read so well, why don't you read
what it says and not ask me so much? Where's
Herbert?"

Herbert is now on the point of pushing over a little case of Etruscan bowls in an attempt to get at the figure of a Bœotian horse in the case behind it.

"Here, Herbert, don't push that like that! Do you want to break it?"

"Yes," replies Herbert, giving you a short answer.

"Well, we'll go right straight home if you are going to act that way." (Here a good idea strikes you: Why *not* go right straight home and blame it on Herbert?)

The first evidences of "Smithsonian feet" are beginning to make themselves felt. You try walking on your ankles to favor the soles of your feet, but that doesn't help. And you haven't even struck the second floor yet.

By actual count, the word "look" has been called out eighty-two times, and each time you have looked. Forty-three questions have been asked, forty of which you have answered incorrectly and thirty-four of which you have been caught answering incorrectly. It is high time that you did go home.

But the boys are just beginning. They spot another room at the end of the wing and rush to it. You trail after them, all your old fire gone. It turns out to be Glacier Hall again.

"We've been in here before," you say, hoping that this will discourage them. "There's the door to the street over there. How about going home and coming again tomorrow?"

You trail after them, all the old fire gone

This suggestion is not even heard, for the boys are on their way up the big flight of stairs leading to the second floor. If you can make half the flight you will be doing well. By the time you reach the first landing, you are in a state of collapse.

"Look, Daddy!" you hear the little voices calling from above. "Come quick, Daddy! Skeletons!"

And skeletons they are, sure enough. Mastodon skeletons. Herbert, turning the corner hurriedly, comes suddenly on one and is thrown into a panic. Not a bad idea! Perhaps they might both be frightened into wanting to go home. But Nature herself comes to your rescue. At the end of the mastodon room Herbert comes and whispers to you.

"I don't know," you reply hopefully. "Perhaps we had better go home."

"No," screams Herbert. "I want to stay here."

"Well, come along with me then, and we'll see if we can find it. Come on, Arthur. Come with Herbert and Daddy."

So, on the pretext of locating the section of the building in question you lead the boys down stairs and out the back way.

"Over here, I guess," you say. "No, I guess over there."

By this time, you are at the street and within hailing distance of a taxi. It is but the work of a minute to hit Herbert over the head until he is quiet and to yank Arthur into the cab along with you.

"Drive quickly to 468 Elm avenue," you say to the driver.

That would be your home address.

Traveling
in Peace

The Uncommercial Traveler and His Problems

EVEN in an off year, the conversational voltage is very high on the trans-Atlantic greyhounds (ocean liners). There is something in the sea air which seems to bring a sort of kelp to the surface even in the most reticent of passengers, and before the ship has passed Fire Island you will have heard as much dull talk as you would get at a dozen Kiwanis meetings at home. And the chances are that you, yourself, will have done nothing that you can be particularly proud of as a raconteur. They tell me that there is something that comes up from the bilge which makes people like that on shipboard.

I myself solved the problem of shipboard conversation by traveling alone and pretending to be a deaf-mute. I recommend this ruse to other irritable souls.

There is no sense in trying to effect it if you have the family along. There is no sense in trying to effect *anything* if you have the family along. But there is something about a family man which seems to attract prospective talkers. Either the Little Woman scrapes up acquaintances who have to have their chairs moved next to yours and tell you all about how rainy it was all spring in East Orange, or the children stop people on the deck and drag them up to you to have you show them how to make four squares out of six matches, and once you have established these contacts, you might as well stay in your stateroom for the rest of the voyage.

Once you are alone, you can then start in on the deaf-mute game. When you go down to dinner, write out your order to the steward and pretty soon the rest of the people at your table will catch on to the fact that something is wrong. You can do a few pleasant passes of sign language if the thing seems to be getting over too slowly. As a matter of fact, once you have taken your seat without remarking on the condition of the ocean to your right-hand neighbor, you will have established yourself as sufficiently queer to be known as "that man at our table who can't talk." Then you probably will be left severely alone.

Once you are out on deck, stand against the rail and look off at the horizon. This is an invitation which few ocean-talkers can resist. Once they see anyone who looks as if he wanted to be alone, they immediately are rarin' to go. One of them will come up to you and look at the horizon with you for a minute, and then will say:

"Isn't that a porpoise off there?"

If you are not very careful you will slip and say: "Where?" This is fatal. What you should do is turn and smile very sweetly and nod your head as if to say: "Don't waste your time, neighbor. I can't

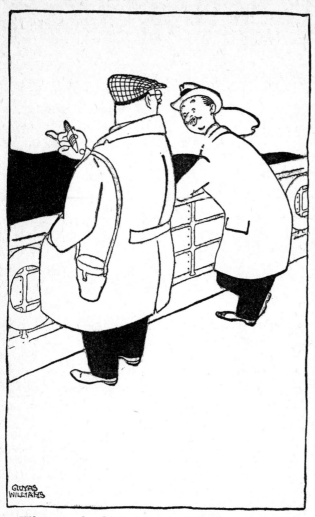

What you should do is turn and smile very sweetly

hear a word you say." Of course, there is no porpoise and the man never thought there was; so he
will immediately drop that subject and ask you if
you are deaf. Here is where you may pull another
bone. You may answer: "Yes, very." That will
get you nowhere, for if he thinks that he can make
you hear by shouting, he will shout. It doesn't
make any difference to him what he has to do to en-
gage you in conversation. He will do it. He would
spell words out to you with alphabet blocks if he
thought he could get you to pay any attention to his
story of why he left Dallas and what he is going to
do when he gets to Paris.

So keep your wits about you and be just the deaf-
est man that ever stepped foot on a ship. Pretty
soon he will get discouraged and will pass on to the
next person he sees leaning over the rail and ask
him if that isn't a "porpoise 'way off there." You
will hear the poor sucker say, "Where?" and then
the dam will break. As they walk off together you
will hear them telling each other how many miles
they get to a gallon and checking up on the comparative sizes of the big department stores in their
respective towns.

After a tour of the smoking-room and writing-
room making deaf-and-dumb signs to the various
stewards, you will have pretty well advertised yourself as a hopeless prospect conversationally. You
may then do very much as you like.

Perhaps not quite as you like. There may be one
or two slight disadvantages to this plan. There may
be one or two people on board to whom you *want*

to speak. Suppose, for instance, that you are sitting at one of those chummy writing desks where you look right into the eyes of the person using the other half. And suppose that those eyes turn out to be something elegant; suppose they turn out to be very elegant indeed. What price being dumb then?

Your first inclination, of course, is to lean across

Suppose those eyes turn out to be something elegant

the top of the desk and say: "I beg your pardon, but is this your pen that I am using?" or even more exciting: "I beg your pardon, but is this your letter that I am writing?" Having been posing as a deaf-mute up until now, this recourse is denied you, and you will have to use some other artifice.

There is always the old Roman method of writing notes. If you decide on this, just scribble out the following on a bit of ship's stationery: "I may be deaf and I may be dumb, but if you think that makes any difference in the long run, you're crazy." This

160

is sure to attract the lady's attention and give her some indication that you are favorably impressed with her. She may write a note back to you. She may even write a note to the management of the steamship line.

Another good way to call yourself to her attention would be to upset the writing desk. In the general laughter and confusion which would follow, you could grab her and carry her up on deck where you could tell her confidentially that you really were not deaf and dumb but that you were just pretending to be that way in order to avoid talking to people who did not interest you. The fact that you were talking to her, you could point out, was a sure sign that she, alone, among all the people on the ship, *did* interest you; a rather pretty compliment to her, in a way. You could then say that, as it was essential that none of the other passengers should know that you could talk, it would be necessary for her to hold conversations with you clandestinely, up on the boat deck, or better yet, in one of the boats. The excitement of this would be sure to appeal to her, and you would unquestionably become fast friends.

There is one other method by which you could catch her favor as you sat looking at her over the top of the desk, a method which is the right of every man whether he be deaf, dumb or bow-legged. You might wink one eye very slowly at her. It wouldn't be long then before you could tell whether or not it would be worth your while to talk.

However it worked out, you would have had a comparatively peaceful voyage.

The Future of the Class of 1926— North Central Grammar School

Class Prophecy by William N. Crandle, '26

THE other night I had a dream in which I saw all that was going to happen to the Class of 1926 of the North Central Grammar School in the future, and when, much to my surprise, I was elected to be Class Prophet, it occurred to me that it might be a good idea to write down the things I saw in that dream and tell you something of what is going to happen in 1950 to the members of the Class of 1926.

In this dream I happened to be walking down the street when suddenly I saw a familiar face standing on a soap-box at the corner, and in a minute I recognized Harry Washburn, our Class President, who was evidently making some sort of a speech to the assembled multitude, among whom I recognized Edna Gleen, Harriet Mastom and Lillian MacArdle. "Well," I said to myself, "I always knew that those girls were crazy about Harry, and I guess they still are." Harry was making some sort of a speech and I gathered that he was running for President of the United States, which didn't surprise me at all as Harry always was a politician in grammar school days.

A little further along I heard someone making a speech on another corner, and I looked a little closer and saw that it was Beatrice Franley, who was making a speech against the use of face-powder by girls. It seemed that Prohibition had been done away with but that Beatrice was trying to get an amendment to the Constitution preventing girls from using face-powder. "Well," I said to myself, "back in North Central, Beatrice was always rabid on the subject of girls using face-powder and she doesn't seem to have lost it even in 1950." Listening to Beatrice were George Delmot, Bertram Posner and Mary Alley.

A little further along I came to a big sign which said: "William Nevin and Gertrude Dolby, Ice-Cream Parlor," and I remembered that when they were in school William and Gertrude were always eating ice-cream at recess together, so I wasn't much surprised to find that they had gone into the ice-cream business, and it occurred to me that they probably ate more ice-cream than they sold.

Pretty soon I came to a big crowd which was watching a couple of prizefighters fighting, and imagine my surprise to find out that the prizefighters were Louis Wrentham and George DuGrasse, who had evidently gone in for prizefighting. The referee was Mr. Ranser, our old algebra teacher, and I guessed that he would give the decision to George, as George always was a favorite of his and probably still was.

In a little while I found myself in England, and

there I was told that Walter Dodd had been made King of England because he always dressed like a dude in school, and that he had married Miriam Friedburg and had made her Queen of England. The Prince of Wales had fallen off his horse so often that the English people had elected Philip Wasserman to be Prince because he was so good at using ponies in high-school Latin.

In France I found that George Disch, Harry Petro, John Walters, Robert Dimmock, Edwin Le-Favre and Eddie Matsdorf were working in a café together and that Mary Duggan, Louise Creamer, Margaret Penny and Freda Bertel were constant customers. In Germany, Albert Vogle had been chosen Kaiser because he was so bossy.

On the boat coming back I saw William Debney, Stella Blum, Arthur Crandall, Noble MacOnson and Henry Bostwick, all looking older than they did in North Central, but evidently prosperous, and just as I landed in America I woke up and realized that it had all been nothing but a dream.

Fascinating Crimes

3. The Missing Floor

IT HAS often been pointed out that murderers are given to revisiting the scene of their crimes. The case of Edny Pastelle is the only one on record where the scene of the crime revisited the murderer.

Edny Pastelle was a Basque elevator woman who ran one of the first elevators installed in the old Fifth Avenue Hotel, which stood at the corner of Twenty-third Street and Fifth Avenue, New York City. The elevator was of the surrey type, and was pushed from floor to floor by the operator, who was underneath climbing on a ladder. It was Mlle. Pastelle's daily task to hoist such personages as Chauncey M. Depew, Boss Tweed and Harriet Beecher Stowe up to their rooms in the Fifth Avenue Hotel. In fact, she is said to have been Miss Stowe's model for *Uncle Tom* in the novel of that name (with the word "Cabin" added to it).

In the evenings, when Edny Pastelle was not on duty, she carried Punch and Judy shows about town for whoever wanted them. As not many people wanted them, Edny's evenings were pretty much her own.

The evening of July 7, 1891, however, is on record as being not Edny's, but Max Sorgossen's.

Max Sorgossen worked in the Eden Musée, which was situated on Twenty-third Street just below the Fifth Avenue Hotel. His job was to put fresh cuffs on the wax figure of Chester A. Arthur in the Presidential Group. At five o'clock every afternoon he also took "Ajeeb," the mechanical chess player, out in the back yard for his exercise.

At five-thirty on the afternoon in question Max Sorgossen had just knocked off work and was strolling up Twenty-third Street in search of diversion. In the back of his mind was an idea that perhaps he might find another mechanical chess player for "Ajeeb" and a girl for himself and that the four of them might go down to Coney Island for the evening, as the weather was warm. As he passed the service entrance of the Fifth Avenue Hotel he met Edny Pastelle, who was likewise calling it a day. (She called it a *jour*, but that is the Basque of it.)

Edny and Max had known each other in finishing school, and so there seemed no impropriety in his speaking to her and asking her if she knew of a mechanical chess player for "Ajeeb" and if she would look with favor on an evening at Coney.

The two were seen entering a restaurant on Twenty-first Street to talk it over at 6:10. At 9:20 the next morning guests of the hotel, on trying to descend in the elevator, found it stuck between the first and third floors. When the car was finally dislodged, it was found to contain the body of Max Sorgossen. Furthermore, *the second floor, where the elevator should have stopped, was gone!*

Edny Pastelle and Max Sorgossen in the gallery of human fiends and their victims

—Courtesy of John Held, Jr., and Life.

Edny was arrested and the trial took place in the Court of Domestic Relations, since she was a domestic and there had evidently been relations, albeit unfriendly. The prosecuting attorney was a young lawyer named William T. Jerome, later William Travers Jerome. Following is a transcript of the cross-examination:

Q. What did you do after Sorgossen spoke to you on Twenty-third Street?
A. Pardon.
Q. What did you do after Sorgossen spoke to you on Twenty-third Street?
A. Plenty.
Q. Very good, Mr. Bones. And now tell me, why *is* a man with a silk hat on like Mary Queen of Scots?
A. What Scots?
Q. I'm asking *you.*
A. Animal, vegetable or mineral?
Q. Mineral.
A. The tidy on the back of that chair?
Q. No.
A. Cyrus W. Field?
Q. Give up?
A. Three spades.
Q. Double three spades.

At this point, counsel for the defense objected and the case was thrown out into a higher court, where Edny Pastelle was acquitted, or whatever you call it.

It was some thirty years later that the missing second floor of the old Fifth Avenue Hotel was discovered. A workman laying wagers on the sixteenth floor of the Fifth Avenue Building (erected on the site of the old Fifth Avenue Hotel) came across a floor which was neither the fifteenth, sixteenth nor seventeenth. The police were called in and, after several weeks of investigation and grilling, it was identified as the missing floor of the old hotel, the floor at which the little romance of Edny Pastelle had come to such an abrupt end. How it came to be on the sixteenth floor of the Fifth Avenue Building nobody knows. Perhaps Max Sorgossen could tell.

"Howdy,
Neighbor!"

AMONG the inhabitants of North America there
is a queer tribal custom which persists in spite
of being universally unpopular. Its technical name
is "paying a call." The women of the tribe are its
chief priests, but once in a while the men are roped
in on it and it is then that the lamentations and
groans may be heard even in the surrounding vil-
lages.

Among the women-folk the procedure is as follows: The one who is to "pay a call" puts on what
she considers her most effective regalia, collects ten
or a dozen engraved cards bearing her name and
twice that number bearing her husband's (he
doesn't even know that he *has* any cards, let alone
that they are being thrown around the neighborhood every Wednesday afternoon), and sets out with
the bit between her teeth.

The idea is to call on as many other women as
she thinks will not be at home. Ringing the doorbell at each house on her list, she inquires of the
maid if her mistress is in. On receiving a favorable
answer ("No") she drops the required number of
cards and runs down the street to her car or bicycle
or whatever she came in, and rushes off at top speed
lest the maid should suddenly discover that her

mistress is at home after all. The chances are, however, that the maid has had instructions to say "no" from the lady of the house herself, who is at that moment standing at the head of the stairs waiting for the door to shut.

The social amenities having been satisfied in this manner at perhaps ten other houses, the caller returns home, where she sinks into a chair, pulls off her gloves, and sighs: "Thank Heaven, *that's* done!"

It is on those rare occasions when the men of the tribe are impressed into service in this paying of calls that the thing assumes its most horrible aspect. Let us take a peek into a typical celebration of the rite.

The man returns home from the office at night, all set for an evening with a motor-boat catalog in front of the fire.

"I thought we might run up and call on the Grimsers tonight. We've owed them a call for a long time now."

"The Grimsers?" queries the husband.

"Yes, you know them. He's the little short man we saw in the drug-store the other night. She is quite pleasant, but rather fast, I understand. She told me that her husband was very anxious to know you better."

"What is he—in the insurance business?"

"No, he isn't. He's a very nice man. And *she* is just mad about you. 'Mrs. Tomlin,' she said to me, 'you don't mean to tell me that that nice-looking

*On receiving a favorable answer one drops the re-
quired number of cards*

husband of yours is forty years old! He looks about twenty-five. And such nice hair!' "

"Well," says the husband, not unmoved by this bit of strategy, "I suppose if we must, we must. Do I have to get dressed up?"

And so they start out for a call on the Grimsers, with whom they have no more in common than the same milkman.

Their reception is more or less formal in tone, as the Grimsers had planned on going to bed early, Mr. Grimser even having gone so far as his dressing-gown.

"Do sit over here," urges Mrs. Grimser, indicating her husband's favorite cavity in the corner of the divan, "that rocker is so uncomfortable."

"It just suits me," lies Mrs. Tomlin. "Ed says that he is glad that I like chairs like this, as it leaves all the comfortable ones in the house for him."

Everyone looks at Ed as the author of this pleasantry, and there is general, albeit extremely moderate laughter.

"Well, did you ever see such weather?" This might come from anybody. In fact, two or three are likely to say it at once. This leads to an account on the part of Mrs. Grimser of what the dampness has done to her jelly in the cellar, and a story by Mrs. Tomlin illustrating how hard it is to keep a maid contented during a rainy spell. Mr. Tomlin leads off with one he heard at the club about the farmer who prayed for rain, but noticing a sudden tightening of his wife's lips accompanied by a warning tapping of her right foot, he gathers that probably Mrs. Grimser's father was a clergyman or something, and trails his story off into a miserable series of noises.

Trails his story off into a miserable series of noises

This is a signal for Mrs. Grimser to say: "I just know that you men are dying to get off in a corner and talk to each other. Harry, why don't you show Mr. Grimser the plans for the new garage?"

The two men are then isolated on a window-seat, where they smoke and try to think up something to say next. Mr. Tomlin, knowing nothing about blueprints and caring less about the Grimsers' garage, its forced to bend over the sheets and ask unintelligent questions, cooing appreciatively now and then to show that he is getting it. They finally are reduced to checking up on mutual acquaintances in the automobile business, summarizing each new find with: "Yes, sir, George is a great old scout," or "Yes, sir, Nick is a great old scout." Everyone possible having been classified as a great old scout, they just sit and puff in silence, frankly talked out.

They just sit and puff in silence, frankly talked out

The ladies, in the meantime, have been carrying on much the same sort of line, except that each has her eye out for details outside the conversation. Mrs. Grimser is trying to make out just how Mrs.

Tomlin's transformation is tied on, and Mrs. Tomlin is making mental notes of the material in Mrs. Grimser's under-curtains. Given nothing to talk about, women can make a much more convincing stab at it than men. To hear them from a distance, you might almost think that they were really saying something.

When all the contestants are completely worn out and the two men reduced to a state of mental inertia bordering on death, Mrs. Tomlin brightens up and says that they must be going. This throws a great wave of relief over the company, and Mr. Tomlin jumps to his feet and says that he'll run ahead and see if the engine is working all right. The Grimsers very cautiously suggest that it is early yet, but unless the Tomlins are listening very carefully (which they are not) they will not hear it.

Then, all the way home, Mrs. Tomlin suggests that Mr. T. might be a little more agreeable to her friends when they go out of an evening, and Mr. Tomlin wants to know what the hell he did that was wrong.

"You know very well what you did that was wrong, and besides, what a story to start telling in front of Mrs. Grimser!"

"What story?"

"The one about the farmer who prayed for rain."

"What's the matter with that story?"

"You know very well what's the matter with it. You seem to think when you are out with my friends that you are down in the locker-room with George Herbert."

"I wish to God I *was* down in the locker-room with George Herbert."

"Oh, you make me sick."

The rest of the ride home is given over to a stolid listening to the chains clanking on the pavement as the wheels go round.

This is known in the tribe life of North America as being "neighborly," and a whole system has been built up on the tradition. Some day a prophet is going to arise out of some humble family and say, "What's the use?" and the whole thing is going to topple over with a crash and everyone is going to be a lot happier.

A Talk
to Young Men

Graduation Address on "The Decline of Sex"

TO YOU young men who only recently were graduated from our various institutions of learning (laughter), I would bring a message, a message of warning and yet, at the same time, a message of good cheer. Having been out in the world a whole month, it is high time that you learned something about the Facts of Life, something about how wonderfully Nature takes care of the thousand and one things which go to make up what some people jokingly call our "sex" life. I hardly know how to begin. Perhaps "Dear Harry" would be as good a way as any.

You all have doubtless seen, during your walks in the country, how the butterflies and bees carry pollen from one flower to another? It is very dull and you should be very glad that you are not a bee or a butterfly, for where the fun comes in *that* I can't see. However, they think that they are having a good time, which is all that is necessary, I suppose. Some day a bee is going to get hold of a real book on the subject, and from then on there will be mighty little pollen-toting done or I don't know my bees.

Well, anyway, if you have noticed carefully how

the bees carry pollen from one flower to another (and there is no reason why you should have noticed carefully as there is nothing to see), you will have wondered what connection there is between this process and that of animal reproduction. I may as well tell you right now that there is no connection at all, and so your whole morning of bee-stalking has been wasted.

We now come to the animal world. Or rather, first we come to One Hundred and Twenty-fifth Street, but you don't get off there. The animal world is next, and off you get. And what a sight meets your eyes! My, my! It just seems as if the whole world were topsy-turvy.

The next time you are at your grocer's buying gin, take a look at his eggs. They really are some hen's eggs, but they belong to the grocer now, as he has bought them and is entitled to sell them. So they really *are* his eggs, funny as it may sound to anyone who doesn't know. If you will look at these eggs, you will see that each one is *almost* round, but not *quite*. They are more of an "egg-shape." This may strike you as odd at first, until you learn that this is Nature's way of distinguishing eggs from large golf balls. You see, Mother Nature takes no chances. She used to, but she learned her lesson. And that is a lesson that all of you must learn as well. It is called Old Mother Nature's Lesson, and begins on page 145.

Now, these eggs have not always been like this. That stands to reason. They once had something to do with a hen or they wouldn't be called hen's eggs.

181

If they are called duck's eggs, that means that they had something to do with a duck. Who can tell me what it means if they are called "ostrich's eggs"? . . . That's right.

But the egg is not the only thing that had something to do with a hen. Who knows what else there was? . . . That's right.

Now the rooster is an entirely different sort of bird from the hen. It is very proud and has a red crest on the top of his head. This red crest is put there by Nature so that the hen can see the rooster coming in a crowd and can hop into a taxi or make a previous engagement if she wants to. A favorite dodge of a lot of hens when they see the red crest of the rooster making in their direction across the barnyard is to work up a sick headache. One of the happiest and most contented roosters I ever saw was one who had had his red crest chewed off in a fight with a dog. He also wore sneakers.

But before we take up this phase of the question (for it is a question), let us go back to the fish kingdom. Fish are probably the worst example that you can find; in the first place, because they work under water, and in the second, because they don't know anything. You won't find one fish in a million that has enough sense to come in when it rains. They are just stupid, that's all, and nowhere is their stupidity more evident than in their sex life.

Take, for example, the carp. The carp is one of the least promising of all the fish. He has practically no forehead and brings nothing at all to a conversation. Now the mother carp is swimming around some fine spring day when suddenly she decides that it would be nice to have some children. So she makes out a deposit slip and deposits a couple million eggs on a rock (all this goes on *under* water, mind you, of all places). This done, she adjusts her hat, powders her nose, and swims away, a woman with a past.

It is not until all this is over and done with that papa enters the picture, and then only in an official capacity. Papa's job is very casual. He swims over the couple of million eggs and takes a chance that by sheer force of personality he can induce half a dozen of them to hatch out. The remainder either go to waste or are blacked up to represent caviar.

So you will see that the sex life of a fish is nothing much to brag about. It never would present a problem in a fish community as it does in ours. No committees ever have to be formed to regulate it, and about the only way in which a fish can go wrong is through drink or stealing. This makes a fish's life highly unattractive, you will agree, for, after a time, one would get very tired of drinking and stealing.

We have now covered the various agencies of Nature for populating the earth with the lesser forms of life. We have purposely omitted any reference to the reproduction of those unicellular organisms which reproduce by dividing themselves up into two, four, eight, etc., parts without any outside assistance at all. This method is too silly even to discuss.

We now come to colors. You all know that if you mix yellow with blue you get green. You also get green if you mix cherries and milk. (Just kidding. Don't pay any attention.) The derivation of one color from the mixture of two other colors is not generally considered a sexual phenomenon, but that is because the psychoanalysts haven't got around to it yet. By next season it won't be safe to admit that you like to paint, or you will be giving yourself away as an inhibited old uncle-lover and debauchee. The only thing that the sex-psychologists can't read a sexual significance into is trap-shooting, and they are working on that now.

All of which brings us to the point of wondering if it *all* isn't a gigantic hoax. If the specialists fall down on trap-shooting, they are going to begin to doubt the whole structure which they have erected, and before long there is going to be a reaction which will take the form of an absolute negation of sex. An Austrian scientist has already come out with the announcement that there is no such thing as a hundred per cent male or a hundred per cent female. If this is true, it is really a big step forward. It is going to throw a lot of people out of work, but think of the money that will be saved!

And so, young men, my message to you is this: Think the thing over very carefully and examine the evidence with fair-minded detachment. And if you decide that, within the next ten years, sex is going out of style, make your plans accordingly. Why not be pioneers in the new movement?

184

Biography
by Inches

(Such as has recently been done for Keats)

A LIFE OF WILLIAM BODNEY

*Together with an Examination of His Poetry and
Punctuation*

I

GENESIS

THE weather report submitted by the Suffix
Weather Bureau on May 11, 1837, states that
shortly after three in the afternoon there was a
light rain, a precipitation of some .005 inches.
There is a certain sad significance in this technical
statement of the Weather Bureau, for during that
light rain, George and Edna Bodney were married
in the south vestry of Queen's Church.

We know that it was the south vestry because of
a letter written the next day by the Rev. Dr. Morbeling, the rector, to his sister, Mrs. Wrethnam.
"Such a mess, such a mess!" writes Dr. Morbeling.
"The north vestry has been torn up by plumbers
and plasterers for over a week now, throwing all
the business into that dark, damp old south vestry
which is very difficult to work in owing to the

danger of tripping over the litter of kindergarten chairs."

North or south vestry, however, it is certain (and essential) that George and Edna Bodney were married on May 11, 1837, for on May 13, 1837, William Bodney was born.

II

BROOK AND RIVER

Of the boyhood of William Bodney we know but little. He was brought up as most of the boys in Suffix were brought up, except for the fact that he did not go out of doors until he was eleven, and then only to strike at the postman. He was kept in the house so much because of an old prejudice of Edna Bodney's against fireflies.

We catch a glimpse of Bodney's school life, however, in a letter written by Charles Cod, a fellow student at Wimperis School (From the Danker Collection):

"There are lots of fellows here in school," writes Cod; "among them Henry Mamsley, Ralph Dyke, Luther Fennchurch, William Bodney, Philip Massteter and Norman Walsh."

Cod is no doubt accurate in his letter, although a note of personal prejudice which creeps in now and again makes it a little hard to rely on his judgment.

No more trustworthy is Norman Rully, writing to Ashman in 1845 (Arthur's Collection) when he says that Bodney paid "three shillings for a pair of skates." This is unquestionably an error on Rully's part, for skates at that time cost five shillings if they cost a nickel.

III

EARLY POETRY

We first find Bodney displaying his genius on the occasion of the presentaton to him of a knitted necktie by Laura Pensick, the sister of his friend Alan Pensick. The tie was given to him early in the afternoon and by evening the young man had composed the following sonnet in honor of its fair donor:

LINES ON OPENING A LETTER AND FINDING SAND IN IT

When hours of sorry death have thundered by
    And with them open windows to the sea
    Lycurgus from his moss-bedowered tree
Brings asphodel to deck the starry sky.
The winter-scarred olympids homeward fly
    And softly spread their wolden heraldry
    Yet Lacedemon does not wake in fantasy
Nor Thetis sing her songs to such as I.

So, Laura, how shall Eros take his due
    Or crafty Xerxes leave his tent at night
If, dropping down from his cerulean blue,
    He brings not gold with him wherewith to fight?
The ploughman homeward plods his weary way
    And, what is more, you'll be a man, my son.

.   .   .   .   .

187

The boy in Bodney is fading and giving place to the man. This sonnet, while not perfect, shows what was going on in the youth's mind. Of course, "moss-bedowered tree" is bad, and Lacedemon was the name of a country, not a person, but "winter-scarred olympids" makes up for a great deal, and the picture of decking "the starry sky" with asphodel comes doubtless from Bodney's vacation days in Polpero where there are a lot of rocks and seaweed. Henry Willers, in a most interesting paper on *Bodney's Relation to Open Windows*, points out that the "open windows to the sea" probably refers to an old window of his aunt's which she kept upstairs in the house at Ragley. Mr. Willers is probably right also in believing that in line six, the word "their" comes from a remark make by Remson to Bodney concerning some plovers sent him (Remson) after a hunting trip. "I am using *their* feathers," Remson is reported to have said, "to make a watch fob with."

These are fascinating speculations, but we must not linger too long with them. Even as we speculate, the boy Bodney is turning into the man Bodney, and is looking searchingly at the life about him. Poor Bodney! We know now that he looked once too often.

IV

SHOPPING IN LONDON

The first big adventure in William Bodney's life was a trip up to London to buy shoes. The shoes which he had been wearing in Suffix, we learn from the Town Clerk's record, were "good enough," but "good enough" was never a thing to satisfy William Bodney. The fashion at the time was to wear shoes only to parties and coronations, but Bodney was never one to stick to the fashion.

So bright and early on the morning of April 9, 1855, the young man set out for the city, full of the vigor of living. Did he go by coach or by foot? We do not know. On the coach records of April 9, there is a passenger listed as "Enoch Reese," but this was probably not William Bodney. There is no reason why he should have traveled under the name of "Enoch Reese." But whether he went by coach or over the road, we do know that he must have passed through Weeming-on-Downs, as there was no way of getting to London from Suffix without passing through Weeming-on-Downs. And as Bodney went through this little town, probably bright in the sunlight of the early April morning, is it not possible that he stopped at the pump in the square to wet his wrists against the long, hot journey ahead? It is not only possible. It is more than likely. And, stopping at the pump, did he know that in the third house on the left as you leave the pump Londonwards, was Mary Wassermann? Or, did Mary Wassermann know that Bodney was just outside her door? The speculation is futile, for Mary Wassermann moved from Weeming-on-Downs the next week and was never heard from again. But I anticipate.

Of Bodney's stay in London we know but little.

We know that he reached London, for he sent a postcard to his mother from there saying that he had arrived "safe and sound." We know that he left London, because he died fifteen years later in Suffix. What happened in between we can only conjecture at, but we may be sure that he was very sensitive to whatever beauty there may have been in London at that time. In the sonnet *On Looking Into a Stereoscope for the First Time,* written when he had grown into full manhood, we find reference to this visit to the city:

> And, with its regicidal note in tune,
> Brings succor to the waiting stream.

If this isn't a reference to the London trip, what is it a reference to?

V

PROGRESS AND REGRESS

We have seen Bodney standing on the threshold of the Great Experience. How did he meet it? Very well indeed.

For the first time we find him definitely determined to create. "I am definitely determined to create," he wrote to the Tax Collector of Suffix (Author's Collection). And with the spring of 1860 came, in succession, *To Some Ladies Who Have Been Very Nice To Me, Ode to Hester, Rumpty:*

A Fragment, and *To Arthur Hosstetter MacMonigal.* Later in the same year came *I wonder when, if I should go, there'd be.*

It is in *I wonder when, if I should go, there'd be* that Bodney for the first time strikes the intimate note.

> I sometimes think that open fires are best,
> Before drab autumn swings its postern shut . . .

"Open fires" is a delightful thought, carrying with it the picture of a large house, situated on a hill with poplars, the sun sinking charmingly behind the town in the distance and, inside, the big hall, hung with banners, red and gold, and a long table laden with rich food, nuts, raisins, salt (plenty of salt, for Bodney was a great hand to put salt on his food and undoubtedly had salt in mind), and over all the presence of the king and his knights, tall, vigorous blond knights swearing allegiance to their lord. Or perhaps in the phrase Bodney had in mind, a small room with nobody in it. Who can tell? At any rate, we have the words "open fires" and we are able to reconstruct what went on in the poet's mind if we have a liking for that sort of thing. And, although he does not say so in so many words, there is little doubt but that in using "fires" in conjunction with the word "open" he meant Lillian Walf and what was to come later.

VI

MIRAGE

From *I wonder when, if I should go, there'd be* to *On Meeting Roger H. Clafflin for the Second Time* is a far cry—and a merry one. *On Meeting Roger H. Clafflin for the Second Time* is hepta-syllabic and, not only that, but trochaic. Here, after years of suffering and disillusion, after discovering false friends and vain loves, we find Bodney resorting to the trochee. His letter to his sister at the time shows the state of mind the young poet was in (Rast Collection):

Somehow today I feel that things are closing in on me. Life is closing in on me. I have a good mind to employ the trochee and see what that will do. I have no fault to find with the spondee. Some of my best work is spondaic. But I guess there just comes a time in everyone's life when the spondee falls away of its own accord and the trochee takes its place. It is Nature's way. Ah, Nature! How I love Nature! I love the birds and the flowers and Beauty of all kinds. I don't see how anyone can hate Beauty, it is so wonderful. . . . Well, there goes the bell, so I must close now and employ a spondee.

Seven days later Bodney met Lillian Walf.

VII

FINIS ORIGINE PENDET

We do not know whether it was at four o'clock or a quarter past four on October 17, 1874, that

Henry Ryan said to Bodney: "Bodney, I want that you should meet my friend Miss Walf. . . . Miss Walf, Mr. Bodney." The British War Office has no record of the exact hour and Mr. Ryan was blotto at the time and so does not remember. However, it was in or around four o'clock.

Lillian Walf was three years older than Bodney, but had the mind of a child of eight. This she retained all her life. Commentators have referred to her as feeble minded, but she was not feeble minded. Her mind was vigorous. It was the mind of a vigorous child of eight. The fact that she was actually in her thirties has no bearing on the question that I can see. Writing to Remson three years after her marriage to Bodney, Lillian says:

We have a canary which sings something terrible all day. I think I'll shoot it Tuesday.

If that is the product of a feeble mind, then who of us can lay claim to a sound mentality?

The wedding of Bodney to Lillian Walf took place quietly except for the banging of the church radiator. The parson, Rev. Dr. Padderson, estimated that the temperature of the room was about 78° at the time, too hot for comfort. However, the young couple were soon on their way to Bayswater where they settled down and lived a most uneventful life from then on. Bodney must have been quite happy in his new existence, for he gave up writing poetry and took to collecting pewter. We have no record of his ever writing anything after his marriage, except a sonnet for the yearbook of the Bays-water School for Girls. This sonnet (*On Looking into William Ewart Gladstone*) beginning:

O Lesbos! When thy fêted songs shall ring . . .

is too well known to quote here in full, but we cannot help calling attention to the reference to Bayswater. For it was in Bayswater that Bodney really belonged and it was there that he died in 1876. His funeral was a Masonic one and lasted three hours and twenty minutes. (Author's Collection).

Paul Revere's Ride

*How a Modest Go-Getter Did His Bit for the Juno
Acid Bath Corporation*

FOLLOWING are the salesman's report sheets
sent into the home office in New York by
Thaddeus Olin, agent for the Juno Acid Bath Corporation. Mr. Olin had the New England territory
during the spring of 1775 and these report sheets
are dated April 16, 17, 18, and 19, of that year.

> *April 16, 1775.*
> *Boston.*

Called on the following engravers this a. m.:
Boston Engraving Co., E. H. Hosstetter, Theodore
Platney, Paul Revere, Benjamin B. Ashley and
Roger Durgin.

Boston Engraving Co. are all taken care of for
their acid.

E. H. Hosstetter took three tins of acid No. 4
on trial and renewed his old order of 7 Queen-
Biters.

Theodore Platney has gone out of business since
my last trip.

Paul Revere was not in. The man in his shop
said that he was busy with some sort of local shin-
dig. Said I might catch him in tomorrow morning.

The Benjamin Ashley people said they were satisfied with their present product and contemplated no change.

Roger Durgin died last March.

Things are pretty quiet in Boston right now.

April 17.

Called on Boston Engraving people again to see if they might not want to try some Daisy No. 3. Mr. Lithgo was interested and said to come in to-morrow when Mr. Lithgo, Senior, would be there.

Paul Revere was not in. He had been in for a few minutes before the shop opened and had left word that he would be up at Sam Adams' in case anyone wanted him. Went up to the Adams place, but the girl there said that Mr. Revere and Mr. Adams had gone over to Mr. Dawes' place on Milk Street. Went to Dawes' place, but the man there said Dawes and Adams and Revere were in conference. There seems to be some sort of parade or something they are getting up, something to do with the opening of the new foot-bridge to Cambridge, I believe.

Things are pretty quiet here in Boston, except for the trade from the British fleet which is out in the harbour.

Spent the evening looking around in the coffee houses. Everyone here is cribbage-crazy. All they seem to think of is cribbage, cribbage, cribbage.

April 18.

To the Boston Engraving Company and saw Mr.

196

Lithgo, Senior. He seemed interested in the Daisy No. 3 acid and said to drop in again later in the week.

Paul Revere was out. His assistant said that he knew that Mr. Revere was in need of a new batch of acid and had spoken to him about our Vulcan No. 2 and said he might try some. I would have to see Mr. Revere personally, he said, as Mr. Revere makes all purchases himself. He said that he thought I could catch him over at the Dawes' place.

Tried the Dawes' place but they said that he and Mr. Revere had gone over to the livery stable on State Street.

Went to the livery stable but Revere had gone. They said he had engaged a horse for tonight for some sort of entertainment he was taking part in. The hostler said he heard Mr. Revere say to Mr. Dawes that they might as well go up to the North Church and see if everything was all set; so I gather it is a church entertainment.

Followed them up to the North Church, but there was nobody there except the caretaker, who said that he thought I could catch Mr. Revere over at Charlestown late that night. He described him to me so that I would know him and said that he probably would be on horseback. As it seemed to me to be pretty important that we land the Revere order for Vulcan No. 2, I figured out that whatever inconvenience it might cause me to go over to Charlestown or whatever added expense to the firm, would be justified.

Spent the afternoon visiting several printing establishments, but none of them do any engraving.

Things are pretty quiet here in Boston.

Went over to Charlestown after supper and hung around "The Bell in Hand" tavern looking for Mr. Revere. Met a man there who used to live in Peapack, N. J., and we got to talking about what a funny name for a town that was. Another man said that in Massachusetts there was actually a place called Podunk, up near Worcester. We had some very good cheese and talked over names of towns for a while. Then the second man, the one who knew about Podunk, said he had to go as he had a date with a man. After he had left I happened to bring the conversation around to the fact that I was waiting for a Mr. Paul Revere, and the first man told me that I had been talking to him for half an hour and that he had just gone.

I rushed out to the corner, but the man who keeps the watering-trough there said that someone answering Mr. Revere's description had just galloped off on a horse in the direction of Medford. Well, this just made me determined to land that order for Juno Acid Bath Corporation or die in the attempt. So I hired a horse at the Tavern stable and started off toward Medford.

Just before I hit Medford I saw a man standing out in his night-shirt in front of his house looking up the road. I asked him if he had seen anybody who looked like Mr. Revere. He seemed pretty sore and said that some crazy coot had just ridden by and knocked at his door and yelled something that he couldn't understand and that if he caught him he'd break his back. From his description of the horse I gathered that Mr. Revere was the man; so I galloped on.

A lot of people in Medford Town were up and standing in front of their houses, cursing like the one I had just seen. It seems that Mr. Revere had gone along the road-side, knocking on doors and yelling something which nobody understood, and then galloping on again.

"Some god-dam drunk," said one of the Medfordites, and they all went back to bed.

I wasn't going to be cheated out of my order now, no matter what happened, and I don't think that Mr. Revere could have been drunk, because while he was with us at "The Bell in Hand," he had only four short ales. He had a lot of cheese, though.

Something seemed to have been the matter with him, however, because in every town that I rode through I found people just going back to bed after having been aroused up out of their sleep by a mysterious rider. I didn't tell them that it was Mr. Revere, or that it was probably some stunt to do with the shin-dig that he and Mr. Dawes were putting on for the North Church. I figured out that it was a little publicity stunt.

Finally, just as I got into Lexington, I saw my man getting off his horse at a house right alongside the Green. I rushed up and caught him just as he was going in. I introduced myself and told him that I represented the Juno Acid Bath Corporation of New York and asked him if he could give me a few minutes, as I had been following him all the way from Charlestown and had been to his office three days in succession. He said that he was busy right at that minute, but that if I wanted to come along with him upstairs he would talk business on the way. He asked me if I wasn't the man he had been talking to at "The Bell in Hand" and I said yes, and asked him how Podunk was. This got him in good humour and he said that we might as well sit right down then and that he would get someone else to do what he had to do. So he called a man-servant and told him to go right upstairs, wake up Mr. Hancock and Mr. Adams and tell them to get up, and no fooling. "Keep after them, Sambo," he said, "and don't let them roll over and go to sleep again. It's very important."

So we sat down in the living room and I got out our statement of sales for 1774 and showed him that, in face of increased competition, Juno had practically doubled its output. "There must be some reason for an acid outselling its competitors three to one," I said, "and that reason, Mr. Revere, is that a Juno product is a guaranteed product." He asked me about the extra sixpence a tin and I asked him if he would rather pay a sixpence less and get an inferior grade of acid and he said, "No." So I finally landed an order of three dozen tins of Vulcan No. 2 and a dozen jars of

Acme Silver Polish, as Mr. Revere is a silversmith, also, on the side.

Took a look around Lexington before I went back to Boston, but didn't see any engraving plants. Lexington is pretty quiet right now.

Respectfully submitted,
THADDEUS OLIN.

Attached.

Expense Voucher

Juno Acid Bath Corp., New York

Thaddeus Olin, Agent.

Hotel in Boston		15s.
Stage fare		30s.
Meals (4 days)		28s.
Entertaining prospects	£3	4s.
Horse rent. Charlestown to Lexington and return	£2	6s.
Total Expense	£9	3s.
To Profit on three dozen tins of Vulcan No. 2		18s
and One dozen jars Acme Silver Polish		4s.
	£1	2s.
Net Loss	£8	1s.

Shakespeare Explained

Carrying on the System of Footnotes to a Silly Extreme

PERICLES

ACT II. SCENE 3

Enter first Lady-in-Waiting (Flourish,[1] Haut-boys[2] and[3] torches[4]).

First Lady-in-Waiting—What[5] ho![6] Where[7] is[8] the[9] music?[10]

NOTES

1. *Flourish:* The stage direction here is obscure. Clarke claims it should read "flarish," thus changing the meaning of the passage to "flarish" (that is, the King's), but most authorities have agreed that it should remain "flourish," supplying the predicate which is to be flourished. There was at this time a custom in the countryside of England to flourish a mop as a signal to the passing vender of berries, signifying that in that particular household there was a consumer-demand for berries, and this may have been meant in this instance. That Shakespeare was cognizant of this custom of flourishing the mop for berries is shown in a similar passage in the second part of King Henry IV, where

he has the Third Page enter and say, "Flourish."
Cf. also Hamlet, IV, 7:4.

2. *Hautboys*, from the French *haut*, meaning
"high" and the Eng. *boys*, meaning "boys." The
word here is doubtless used in the sense of "high

*Might be one of the hautboys bearing a box of
"trognies" for the actors to suck*

boys," indicating either that Shakespeare intended
to convey the idea of spiritual distress on the part
of the First Lady-in-Waiting or that he did not. Of
this Rolfe says: "Here we have one of the chief in-
dications of Shakespeare's knowledge of human nature, his remarkable insight into the petty foibles

203

of this work-a-day world." Cf. T. N. 4:6, "Mine eye hath play'd the painter, and hath stell'd thy beauty's form in table of my heart."

3. *and.* A favorite conjunctive of Shakespeare's in referring to the need for a more adequate navy for England. Tauchnitz claims that it should be pronounced "und," stressing the anti-penult. This interpretation, however, has found disfavor among most commentators because of its limited signif-icance. We find the same conjunctive in A. W. T. E. W. 6:7, "Steel-boned, unyielding *and* uncomplying virtue," and here there can be no doubt that Shake-speare meant that if the King should consent to the marriage of his daughter the excuse of Stephano, offered in Act 2, would carry no weight.

4. *Torches.* The interpolation of some foolish player and never the work of Shakespeare (Warb.). The critics of the last century have disputed whether or not this has been misspelled in the orig-inal, and should read "trochies" or "troches." This might well be since the introduction of tobacco into England at this time had wrought havoc with the speaking voices of the players, and we might well imagine that at the entrance of the First Lady-in-Waiting there might be perhaps one of the haut-boys mentioned in the preceding passage bearing a box of "troches" or "trognies" for the actors to suck. Of this entrance Clarke remarks: "The noble mixture of spirited firmness and womanly modesty, fine sense and true humility, clear sagacity and absence of conceit, passionate warmth and sensi-

tive delicacy, generous love and self-diffidence with which Shakespeare has endowed this First Lady-in-Waiting renders her in our eyes one of the most admirable of his female characters." Cf. M. S. N. D. 8:9, "That solder'st close impossibilities and mak'st them kiss."

5. *What*—What.

6. *Ho!* In conjunction with the preceding word doubtless means "What ho!" changed by Clarke to "what hoo!" In the original MS. it reads "What hi!" but this has been accredited to the tendency of the time to write "What hi" when "what ho" was meant. Techner alone maintains that it should read "What humpf!" Cf. Ham. 5:0, "High-ho!"

7. *Where.* The reading of the folio, retained by Johnson, the Cambridge editors and others, but it is not impossible that Shakespeare wrote "why," as Pope and others give it. This would make the passage read "Why the music?" instead of "Where is the music?" and would be a much more probable interpretation in view of the music of that time. Cf. George Ade. Fable No. 15, "Why the gunny-sack?"

8. *is*—is not. That is, would not be.

9. *the.* Cf. Ham. 4:6. M. S. N. D. 3:5. A. W. T. E. W. 2:6. T. N. 1:3 and Macbeth 3:1, "that knits up *the* raveled sleeves of care."

10. *music.* Explained by Malone as "the art of making music" or "music that is made." If it has but one of these meanings we are inclined to think it is the first; and this seems to be favored by what

precedes, *"the* music!" Cf. M. of V. 4:2, "The man that hath no music in himself."

The meaning of the whole passage seems to be that the First Lady-in-Waiting has entered, concomitant with a flourish, hautboys and torches and says, "What ho! Where is the music?"

Fascinating Crimes

4. The Lynn Horse-Car Murders

EARLY in the morning of August 7th, 1896, a laborer named George Raccid, while passing the old street-car barns at Fleeming and Main Streets, Lynn, Massachusetts, noticed a crowd of conductors and drivers (horse-cars were all the rage in 1896) standing about a car in the doorway to the barn. Mr. Raccid was too hurried to stop and see what the excitement was, and so it was not until the following Wednesday, when the bi-weekly paper came out, that he learned that a murder had been committed in the car-barn. And at this point, Mr. Raccid drops out of our story.

The murder in question was a particularly odd one. In the first place, it was the victim who did the killing. And in the second, the killing occurred in a horse-car, an odd conveyance at best. And finally, the murderer had sought to conceal his handiwork by cramming his victim into the little stove in the middle of the car, a feat practically impossible without the aid of scissors and a good eye for snipping.

The horse-car in which the murder occurred was one of the older types, even for a horse-car. It was known in the trade as one of the "chummy roadster" models and was operated by one man only.

This man drove the horses, stoked the fire, and collected the fares. He also held the flooring of the car together with one foot braced against a "master" plank. On his day off he read quite a lot.

The murder-car and its driver, Swelf Yoffsen
—Courtesy of John Held, Jr., and **Life.**

The driver of the murder-car was named Swelf Yoffsen, a Swedish murder-car driver. He had come to this country four years before, but, not liking it here, had returned to Sweden. It is not known how he happened to be back in Lynn at this late date.

If we have neglected to state the name of the victim thus far, it is because nobody seemed able to identify him. Some said that he was Charlie Ross, who had disappeared shortly before. Others (the witty ones) said it was Lon Chaney. A vote taken among all those present designated him as the one least likely to succeed.

An interesting feature of this crime was that it

was the sixth of a series of similar crimes, all of which had occurred in Swelf Yoffsen's horse-car. In the other five cases, the victims had been found inadequately packed in the stove at the end of the run, but as Yoffsen, on being questioned, had denied all knowledge of how they got there, the matter had been dropped. After the discovery of the sixth murder, however, Yoffsen was held on a technical charge of homicide.

The trial was one of the social events of the Lynn Mi-Careme season. Yoffsen, on the stand, admitted that the victim was a passenger in his car; in fact, that he was the only passenger. He had got on at the end of the line and had tried to induce Yoffsen to keep on going in the same direction, even though the tracks stopped there. He wanted to see a man in Maine, he had said. But Yoffsen, according to his own story, had refused and had turned his horses around and started for Lynn again. The next he saw of him, people were trying to get him out of the stove. It was Yoffsen's theory that the man, in an attempt to get warm, had tried to crowd his way into the stove and had smothered. On being reminded that the affair took place during a very hot week in August, Yoffsen said that no matter how hot it got during the day in Lynn, the nights were always cool.

Attorney Hammis, for the State, traced the movements of Yoffsen on the morning of the murder and said that they checked up with his movements on the occasions of the five other murders.

He showed that Yoffsen, on each occasion, had stopped the horse-car at a particularly lonely spot and asked the occupants if they minded making a little detour, as there was a bad stretch of track ahead. He had then driven his horses across a cornfield and up a nearby hill on the top of which, in the midst of a clump of bayberry bushes, stood a deserted house. He pointed out that on four out of the six occasions Yoffsen had driven his horses right into the house and asked the passengers (when there were any, other than his victim) if they would step into the front room for a few minutes, giving them some magazines to read while they waited. According to the testimony of seven of these passengers, after about fifteen minutes Yoffsen had appeared and yelled "All aboard!" in a cheery voice and everyone had piled back into the horse-car and away they had gone, over the cornfield and down the hill to Lynn. It was noted that on each occasion, one of the passengers was missing, and that, oddly enough, this very passenger was always the one to be found in the stove on the way back.

It was the State's contention that Yoffsen killed his victims for their insurance, *which is double when the deceased has met his death in a common carrier.*

On April 14th, the ninth day of the trial, the jury went out and shortly after asked for a drink of water. After eighteen hours of deliberation they returned with a verdict of guilty, but added that, as it was not sure whether Yoffsen had actually killed his victims *in* the car or had killed them outside and *then* stuffed them in the stove, he was not entitled to the double insurance.

When they went to inform Yoffsen of the verdict, he was nowhere to be found.

What College Did to Me

M Y COLLEGE education was no haphazard affair. My courses were all selected with a very definite aim in view, with a serious purpose in mind—no classes before eleven in the morning or after two-thirty in the afternoon, and nothing on Saturday at all. That was my slogan. On that rock was my education built.

As what is known as the Classical Course involved practically no afternoon laboratory work, whereas in the Scientific Course a man's time was never his own until four p. m. anyway, I went in for the classic. But only such classics as allowed for a good sleep in the morning. A man has his health to think of. There is such a thing as being a studying fool.

In my days (I was a classmate of the founder of the college) a student could elect to take any courses in the catalogue, provided no two of his choices came at the same hour. The only things he was not supposed to mix were Scotch and gin. This was known as the Elective System. Now I understand that the boys have to have, during the four years, at least three courses beginning with the same letter. This probably makes it very awkward for those who like to get away of a Friday afternoon for the week-end.

Under the Elective System my schedule was somewhat as follows:

Mondays, Wednesdays and Fridays at 11:00:
 Botany 2a (The History of Flowers and Their Meaning)
Tuesdays and Thursdays at 11:00:
 English 26 (The Social Life of the Minor Sixteenth Century Poets)
Mondays, Wednesdays and Fridays at 12:00:
 Music 9 (History and Appreciation of the Clavichord)
Tuesdays and Thursdays at 12:00:
 German 12b (Early Minnesingers—Walter von Vogelweider, Ulric Glannsdorf and Freimann von Stremhofen. Their Songs and Times)
Mondays, Wednesdays and Fridays at 1:30:
 Fine Arts 6 (Doric Columns: Their Uses, History and Various Heights)
Tuesdays and Thursdays at 1:30:
 French 1c (Exceptions to the verb *être*)

This was, of course, just one year's work. The next year I followed these courses up with supplementary courses in the history of lace-making, Russian taxation systems before Catharine the Great, North American glacial deposits and Early Renaissance etchers.

This gave me a general idea of the progress of civilization and a certain practical knowledge which has stood me in good stead in thousands of ways since my graduation.

My system of studying was no less strict. In lecture courses I had my notebooks so arranged that one-half of the page could be devoted to drawings of five-pointed stars (exquisitely shaded), girls' heads, and tick-tack-toe. Some of the drawings in

Some of the drawings in my economics notebook were the finest things I have ever done

my economics notebook in the course on Early English Trade Winds were the finest things I have ever done. One of them was a whole tree (an oak) with every leaf in perfect detail. Several instructors commented on my work in this field.

These notes I would take home after the lecture, together with whatever supplementary reading the course called for. Notes and textbooks would then be placed on a table under a strong lamplight. Next came the sharpening of pencils, which would take perhaps fifteen minutes. I had some of the best sharpened pencils in college. These I placed on the table beside the notes and books.

At this point it was necessary to light a pipe, which involved going to the table where the tobacco was. As it so happened, on the same table was a poker hand, all dealt, lying in front of a vacant chair. Four other chairs were oddly enough occupied by students, also preparing to study. It therefore resolved itself into something of a seminar, or group conference, on the courses under discussion. For example, the first student would say:

"I can't open."

The second student would perhaps say the same thing.

The third student would say: "I'll open for fifty cents."

And the seminar would be on.

At the end of the seminar, I would go back to my desk, pile the notes and books on top of each other, put the light out, and go to bed, tired but happy in the realization that I had not only spent the evening busily but had helped put four of my friends through college.

An inventory of stock acquired at college discloses the following bits of culture and erudition which have nestled in my mind after all these years.

THINGS I LEARNED FRESHMAN YEAR

1. Charlemagne either died or was born or did something with the Holy Roman Empire in 800.

2. By placing one paper bag inside another paper bag you can carry home a milk shake in it.

3. There is a double l in the middle of "parallel."

4. Powder rubbed on the chin will take the place of a shave if the room isn't very light.

5. French nouns ending in "aison" are feminine.

6. Almost everything you need to know about a subject is in the encyclopedia.

7. A tasty sandwich can be made by spreading peanut butter on raisin bread.

8. A floating body displaces its own weight in the liquid in which it floats.

9. A sock with a hole in the toe can be worn inside out with comparative comfort.

10. The chances are against filling an inside straight.

11. There is a law in economics called *The Law of Diminishing Returns,* which means that after a

certain margin is reached returns begin to diminish. This may not be correctly stated, but there *is* a law by that name.

12. You begin tuning a mandolin with **A** and tune the other strings from that.

1. **A** good imitation of measles rash can be effected by stabbing the forearm with a stiff whiskbroom.

2. Queen Elizabeth was not above suspicion.

3. In Spanish you pronounce z like th.

4. Nine-tenths of the girls in a girls' college are not pretty.

5. You can sleep undetected in a lecture course by resting the head on the hand as if shading the eyes.

6. Weakness in drawing technique can be hidden by using a wash instead of black and white line.

7. Quite a respectable bun can be acquired by smoking three or four pipefuls of strong tobacco when you have no food in your stomach.

8. The ancient Phœnicians were really Jews, and got as far north as England where they operated tin mines.

9. You can get dressed much quicker in the morning if the night before when you are going to bed you take off your trousers and underdrawers at once, leaving the latter inside the former.

1. Emerson left his pastorate because he had some argument about communion.

2. All women are untrustworthy.

3. Pushing your arms back as far as they will go fifty times each day increases your chest measurement.

4. Marcus Aurelius had a son who turned out to be a bad boy.

5. Eight hours of sleep are not necessary.

6. Heraclitus believed that fire was the basis of all life.

7. A good way to keep your trousers pressed is to hang them from the bureau drawer.

8. The chances are that you will never fill an inside straight.

9. The Republicans believe in a centralized government, the Democrats in a de-centralized one.

10. It is not necessarily effeminate to drink tea.

SENIOR YEAR

1. A dinner coat looks better than full dress.

2. There is as yet no law determining what constitutes trespass in an airplane.

3. Six hours of sleep are not necessary.

4. Bicarbonate of soda taken before retiring makes you feel better the next day.

5. You needn't be fully dressed if you wear a cap and gown to a nine-o'clock recitation.

6. Theater tickets may be charged.

7. Flowers may be charged.
8. May is the shortest month in the year.

The foregoing outline of my education is true enough in its way, and is what people like to think about a college course. It has become quite the cynical thing to admit laughingly that college did one no good. It is part of the American Credo that all that the college student learns is to catch punts and dance. I had to write something like that to satisfy the editors. As a matter of fact, I learned a great deal in college and have those four years to thank for whatever I know today.

(The above note was written to satisfy those of my instructors and financial backers who may read this. As a matter of fact, the original outline is true, and I had to look up the date about Charlemagne at that.)

Uncle Edith's
Ghost Story

"TELL us a ghost story, Uncle Edith," cried all the children late Christmas afternoon when everyone was cross and sweaty.

"Very well, then," said Uncle Edith, "it isn't much of a ghost story, but you will take it—and like it," he added, cheerfully. "And if I hear any whispering while it is going on, I will seize the luckless offender and baste him one.

"Well, to begin, my father was a poor wood-chopper, and we lived in a charcoal-burner's hut in the middle of a large, dark forest."

"That is the beginning of a fairy story, you big sap," cried little Dolly, a fat, disagreeable child who never should have been born, "and what we wanted was a *ghost* story."

"To be sure," cried Uncle Edith, "what a stupid old woopid I was. The ghost story begins as follows:

"It was late in November when my friend Warrington came up to me in the club one night and said: 'Craige, old man, I want you to come down to my place in Whoopshire for the week-end. There is greffle shooting to be done and grouse no end. What do you say?'

"I had been working hard that week, and the

prospect pleased. And so it was that the 3:40 out of Charing Cross found Warrington and me on our way into Whoopshire, loaded down with guns, plenty of flints, and two of the most beautiful snootfuls ever accumulated in Merrie England.

"It was getting dark when we reached Breeming Downs, where Warrington's place was, and as we drove up the shadowy path to the door, I felt Warrington's hand on my arm.

" 'Cut that out!' I ordered, peremptorily. 'What is this I'm getting into?'

" 'Sh-h-h!' he replied, and his grip tightened. With one sock I knocked him clean across the seat. There are some things which I simply will not stand for.

"He gathered himself together and spoke. 'I'm sorry,' he said. 'I was a bit unnerved. You see, there is a shadow against the pane in the guest room window.'

" 'Well, what of it?' I asked. It was my turn to look astonished.

"Warrington lowered his voice. 'Whenever there is a shadow against the windowpane as I drive up with a guest, that guest is found dead in bed the next morning—dead from fright,' he added, significantly.

"I looked up at the window toward which he was pointing. There, silhouetted against the glass, was the shadow of a gigantic man. I say, 'a man,' but it was more the figure of a large weasel except for a fringe of dark-red clappers that it wore suspended from its beak."

"How do you know they were dark red," asked little Tom-Tit, "if it was the shadow you saw?"

"You shut your face," replied Uncle Edith. "I could hardly control my astonishment at the sight of this thing, it was so astonishing. 'That is in my room?' I asked Warrington.

" 'Yes,' he replied, 'I am afraid that it is.'

"I said nothing, but got out of the automobile and collected my bags. 'Come on,' I announced cheerfully, 'I'm going up and beard Mr. Ghost in his den.'

"So up the dark, winding stairway we went into the resounding corridors of the old seventeenth-century house, pausing only when we came to the door which Warrington indicated as being the door to my room. I knocked.

"There was a piercing scream from within as we pushed the door open. But when we entered, we found the room empty. We searched high and low, but could find no sign of the man with the shadow. Neither could we discover the source of the terrible scream, although the echo of it was still ringing in our ears.

" 'I guess it was nothing,' said Warrington, cheerfully. 'Perhaps the wind in the trees,' he added.

" 'But the shadow on the pane?' I asked.

"He pointed to a fancily carved piece of guest soap on the washstand. 'The light was behind that,' he said, 'and from outside it looked like a man.'

222

" 'To be sure,' I said, but I could see that War-rington was as white as a sheet.

" 'Is there anything that you need?' he asked. 'Breakfast is at nine—if you're lucky,' he added, jokingly.

" 'I think that I have everything,' I said. 'I will do a little reading before going to sleep, and perhaps count my laundry. . . . But stay,' I called him back, 'you might leave that revolver which I see sticking out of your hip pocket. I may need it more than you will.'

"He slapped me on the back and handed me the revolver as I had asked. 'Don't blow into the barrel,' he giggled, nervously.

" 'How many people have died of fright in this room?' I asked, turning over the leaves of a copy of *Town and Country*.

" 'Seven,' he replied. 'Four men and three women.'

" 'When was the last one here?'

" 'Last night,' he said.

" 'I wonder if I might have a glass of hot water with my breakfast,' I said. 'It warms your stomach.'

" 'Doesn't it though?' he agreed, and was gone.

"Very carefully I unpacked my bag and got into bed. I placed the revolver on the table by my pillow. Then I began reading.

"Suddenly the door to the closet at the farther end of the room opened slowly. It was in the shadows and so I could not make out whether there

223

was a figure or not. But nothing appeared. The door shut again, however, and I could hear footfalls coming across the soft carpet toward my bed. A chair which lay between me and the closet was upset as if by an unseen hand, and, simultaneously, the window was slammed shut and the shade pulled down. I looked, and there, against the shade, as if thrown from the *outside*, was the same shadow that we had seen as we came up the drive that afternoon."

"I have to go to the bathroom," said little Roger, aged six, at this point.

"Well, go ahead," said Uncle Edith. "You know where it is."

"I don't want to go alone," whined Roger.

"Go with Roger, Arthur," commanded Uncle Edith, "and bring me a glass of water when you come back."

"And whatever was this horrible thing that was in your room, Uncle Edith?" asked the rest of the children in unison when Roger and Arthur had left the room.

"I can't tell you that," replied Uncle Edith, "for I packed my bag and got the 9:40 back town."

"That is the lousiest ghost story I have ever heard," said Peterkin.

And they all agreed with him.

More Songs for Meller

AS SENORITA RAQUEL MELLER sings entirely in Spanish, it is again explained, the management prints little synopses of the songs on the program, telling what each is all about and why she is behaving the way she is. They make delightful reading during those periods when Señorita Meller is changing mantillas, and, in case she should run out of songs before she runs out of mantillas, we offer a few new synopses for her repertoire.

(1) ¿ Voy Bien?
(AM I GOING IN THE RIGHT DIRECTION?)

When the acorns begin dropping in Spain there is an old legend that for every acorn which drops there is a baby born in Valencia. This is so silly that no one pays any attention to it now, not even the gamekeeper's daughter, who would pay attention to anything. She goes from house to house, ringing doorbells and then running away. She hopes that some day she will ring the right doorbell and will trip and fall, so that Prince Charming will catch her. So far, no one has even come to the door. Poor Pepita! if that is her name.

(2) Camisetas de Flanela
(flannel vests)

Princess Rosamonda goes nightly to the Puerta del Sol to see if the early morning edition of the papers is out yet. If it isn't she hangs around humming to herself. If it is, she hangs around humming just the same. One night she encounters a young matador who is returning from dancing school. The finches are singing and there is Love in the air. Princess Rosamonda ends up in the Police Station.

(3) La Guia
(the time-table)

It is the day of the bull fight in Madrid. Everyone is cock-eyed. The bull has slipped out by the back entrance to the arena and has gone home, disgusted. Nobody notices that the bull has gone except Nina, a peasant girl who has come to town that day to sell her father. She looks with horror at the place in the Royal Box where the bull ought to be sitting and sees there instead her algebra teacher whom she had told that she was staying at home on account of a sick headache. You can imagine her feelings!

(4) No Puedo Comer Eso
(i can not eat that!)

A merry song of the Alhambra—of the Alhambra in the moonlight—of a girl who danced over the wall and sprained her ankle. Lititia is the ward of grouchy old Pampino, President of the First National Banco. She has never been allowed further away than the edge of the piazza because she teases people so. Her lover has come to see her and finds that she is fast asleep. He considers that for once he has the breaks, and tiptoes away without waking her up. Along about eleven o'clock she awakes, and is sore as all get-out.

(5) La Lavandera
(the laundryman)

A coquette, pretending to be very angry, bites off the hand of her lover up to the wrist. Ah, naughty Cirinda! Such antics! However does she think she can do her lessons if she gives up all her time to love-making? But Cirinda does not care. Heedless, heedless Cirinda!

(6) Abra Vd. Esa Ventana
(open that window)

The lament of a mother whose oldest son is too young to vote. She walks the streets singing: "My son can not vote! My son is not old enough!" There seems to be nothing that can be done about it.

The Boys' Camp Business

THERE seems to be an idea prevalent among parents that a good way to solve the summer problem for the boy is to send him to a boys' camp. At any rate, the idea seems to be prevalent in the advertising pages of the magazines.

If all the summer camps for boys and girls turn out the sterling citizens-in-embryo that they claim to do, the future of this country is as safe as if it were in the hands of a governing board consisting of the Twelve Apostles. From the folders and advertisements, we learn that "Camp Womagansett —in the foothills of the White Mountains" sends yearly into the world a bevy of "strong, manly boys, ready for the duties of citizenship and equipped to face life with a clear eye and a keen mind." It doesn't say anything about their digestions, but I suppose they are in tiptop shape, too.

The outlook for the next generation of mothers is no less dazzling. "Camp Wawilla for Girls," we learn, pays particular attention to the spiritual development of Tomorrow's Women and compared to the civic activities of the majority of alumnæ of Wawilla, those of Florence Nightingale or Frances Willard would have to be listed under the head of "Junior Girls' Work."

Holding you under water until you are as good as drowned

Now this is all very splendid, and it is comforting to think that when every boy and girl goes to Womagansett or Wawilla there will be no more Younger Generation problem and probably no crime waves worth mentioning. But there are several other features that go hand in hand with sending the boy to camp which I would like to take up from the parents' point of view, if I may. I will limit myself to twenty minutes.

In the first place, when your boy comes home from camp he is what is known in the circular as "manly and independent." This means that when you go swimming with him he pushes you off the raft and jumps on your shoulders, holding you under water until you are as good as drowned— better, in fact. Before he went to camp, you used to take a kindly interest in his swimming and tell him to "take your time, take it easy," with a feeling of superiority which, while it may have had no foundation in your own natatorial prowess, nevertheless was one of the few points of pride left to you in your obese middle-age. After watching one of those brown heroes in one-piece suits and rubber helmets dive off a tower and swim under water to the raft and back, there was a sort of balm in being able to turn to your son and show him how to do the crawl stroke, even though you yourself weren't one of the seven foremost crawl experts in the country. You could do it better than your son could, and that was something.

It was also very comforting to be able to stand

on the springboard and say: "Now watch Daddy. See? Hands like this, bend your knees. See?" The fact that such exhibitions usually culminated in your landing heavily on the area bounded by the knees and the chest was embarrassing, perhaps, but at that you weren't quite so bad as the boy when he tried the same thing.

But after a summer at camp, the "manly, independent" boy comes back and makes you look like Horace Greeley in his later years. "Do this one, Dad!" he says, turning a double flip off the springboard and cutting into the water like a knife blade. If you try it, you sprain your back. If you don't try it, your self-respect and prestige are shattered. The best thing to do is not to hear him. You can do this by disappearing under the surface every time it looks as if he were going to pull a new one. After a while, however, this ruse gets you pretty soggy and waterlogged and you might better just go in and get dressed as rapidly as possible.

The worst phase of this new-found "independence" is the romping instinct that seems to be developed to a high state of obnoxiousness at all boys' camps. I went to camp when I was a boy, but I don't remember being as unpleasant about my fun as boys today seem to be. I have done many mean things in my time. I have tortured flies and kicked crutches out from under cripples' arms. But I have never, so help me, Confucius, pushed anybody off a raft or come up behind anyone in the water and

"Now watch Daddy. See? Hands like this, bend your knees. See?"

jumped up on his shoulders. And I don't think that Lincoln ever did, either.

There is evidently a course in raft pushing and back jumping in boys' camps today. Those photographs that you see in the camp advertisements, if you examine them closely, will disclose, in nine cases out of ten, a lot of boys pushing each other off rafts. You can't see the ones who are jumping on others' shoulders, as they are under water. But I want to serve notice right now that the next boy who pushes me off a raft when I am not looking, or tries to play leapfrog over me in ten feet of water, is going to be made practically useless as Tomorrow's Citizen, and I am going to do it myself, too. If it happens to be my own son, it will just make the affair the sadder.

Another thing that these manly boys learn at camp is a savage habit of getting up at sunrise. The normal, healthy boy should be a very late sleeper. Who does not remember in his own normal, healthy boyhood having to be called three, four, or even five times in the morning before it seemed sensible to get up? One of the happiest memories of childhood is that of the maternal voice calling up from downstairs, fading away into silence, and the realization that it would be possibly fifteen minutes before it called again.

All this is denied to the boy who goes to a summer camp. When he comes home, he is so steeped in the pernicious practice of early rising that he can't shake it off. Along about six o'clock in the

morning he begins dropping shoes and fixing up
a new stand for the radio in his room. Then he
goes out into the back yard and practices tennis
shots up against the house. Then he runs over a
few whistling arrangements of popular songs and

*You'd be surprised at the sound two bicycle wheels can
make on a gravel path*

rides his bicycle up and down the gravel path.
You would be surprised at the sound two bicycle
wheels can make on a gravel path at six-thirty in
the morning. A forest fire might make the same
crackling sound, but you probably wouldn't be
having a forest fire out in your yard at six-thirty
in the morning. Not if you had any sense, you
wouldn't.

Just what the boys do at camp when they get up

at six is a mystery. They seem to have some sort of setting-up exercises and a swim—more pushing each other off the raft—but they could do that by getting up at eight and still have a good long day ahead of them. I never knew anyone yet who got up at six who did anything more useful between that time and breakfast than banging a tennis ball up against the side of the house, waiting for the civilized members of the party to get up. We have to do enough waiting in this life without getting up early to wait for breakfast.

Next summer I have a good mind to run a boys' camp of my own. It will be on Lake Chabonagog-chabonagogchabonagungamog—yes, there is, too, in Webster, Massachusetts—and I will call it Camp Chabonagogchabonagogchabonagungamog f o r Manly Boys. And by the word "manly," I will mean "like men." In other words, everyone shall sleep just as long as he wants, and when he does get up there will be no depleting "setting-up" exercises. The day will be spent just as the individual camper gosh-darned pleases. No organized "hikes" —I'd like a word on the "hike" problem some day, too—no camp spirit, no talk about Tomorrow's Manhood, and *no pushing people off rafts.*

Goethe's
Love Life

LOVERS of Goethe will rejoice in the recently discovered series of letters which have been added to the world's collection of Goethiana by Dr. Heimsatz Au of Leipzig.

Dr. Au had spent fifteen years searching through bureau-drawers and things for these missing links in the chain of the poet's love-life, and was at last rewarded by finding them in the pocket of an old raincoat belonging to Hugo Kranz. Goethe had evidently given them to Kranz to mail, and the lovable old fellow had completely forgotten them. So the letters were never received by the people to whom they were addressed, which accounts for several queer things that happened subsequently, among them the sudden birth of a daughter in the family of Walter Tierney.

We must remember that at the time these letters were written, Goethe was in delicate health and had seriously contemplated suicide. At least, that was what he said. More likely he was just fooling, as there is no record that he ever succeeded. At any rate, not the Goethe of whom we are speaking. There was a George Goethe who committed suicide in Paris in 1886, but it is doubtful if he was the poet. The first of the Au collection of letters was

written on August 11, 1760, four days after Goethe
had returned from his operation. It was addressed
to Leopold Katz, his old room-mate in the Kindergarten. ". . . I have never been so sore at anyone
in my life," writes Goethe, "as I was at Martha last
Friday."

In closing Goethe promised to send Katz the flow-
ered slippers he had promised him and bade him be
"a good boys (*ein gutes Kind*)."

On November 26 he wrote to the Gebrüder Fei-
genspan, Importers of Fine Mechanical Toys, 1364
Ludwigstrasse, München:

"Gentlemen. . . . On September 12, I sent you
a letter, together with fifteen cents in stamps, re-
questing that you send me for inspection one of
your wheeled ducks as per your advertisement. Our
Herr Rothapfel informs me that the shipment has
never reached us. It is not the money that I object
to, as fifteen cents in stamps is only fifteen cents
in stamps, no matter how you should look at it,
but it strikes me as very funny that a firm of your
standing should be so sloppy in its business transac-
tions. Please oblige."

That is all. Not a word of his heart-aches. Not a
word of his emotional crises. Not a word of Elsa
von Bahnhoff. In fact, not a word about anything
but the wheeled duck. No wonder that, in January,
we find him writing piteously to Lena Lewis, his
teacher:

". . . Well, Lena, this is a fine sort of a day I
must say. Rain, rain, rain, is about all it seems to

know how to do in this dump. And the food. Say!
The worst you ever see (*sehen*)."

Thus we are able to piece together those years
of Goethe's life when he was in a formative frame
of mind and facing his first big problems. In the
light of these letters several of the passages in
"*Dichtung und Wahrheit*" which have hitherto
been clouded in mystery may now be read with a
clearer understanding. We cannot thank Dr. Au
too much—if at all.

Old Program
from the Benchley Collection

*A Glance Backward in the Manner of the Authors of
Theatrical Reminiscences*

FEW, probably, of my readers, will remember
the time when the old Forrest Theater stood
where the Central Park Reservoir now is. In those
days, Central Park was considered 'way downtown,
or "crosstown," as they called it then, and one of
the larks of the period was going "down to Central
Park to see the turtles." There was a large turtle
farm in the Park at that time, run by Anderson M.
Ferderber, and it was this turtle farm, expanding
and growing as the turtles became more venture-
some, which later became the Zoological Exhibit.

I remember very well the night when it was
announced at the Forrest Theater that the building was to be torn down to make way for the new
Reservoir. It was, as I recall, H. M. Ramus
("Henry" Ramus) who made the announcement.
He was playing *Laertes* at the time (*Laertes* was
played with the deuces wild and a ten-cent limit)
when the manager of the theater (Arthur Semden,
who later became Harrison Blashforth) came into
the dressing-room and said: "Well, boys, it's all
over. They're going to build the Reservoir here!"

There was a silence for a full minute—probably more, for the manager had come into the wrong dressing-room and there was nobody there.

At any rate, "Henry" Ramus was selected to go out and tell the audience. He did it with infinite tact, explaining that there was no need for alarm or panic, as the water could not possibly be let in until the theater was down and the Reservoir constructed, but the audience was evidently taking no chances on being drowned, for within three minutes from the time Ramus began speaking everyone in the theater was outdoors and in a hansom cab. Audience psychology is a queer thing, and possibly this audience knew best. At any rate, the old Forrest Theater is no more.

Speaking of "Henry" Ramus, an amusing anecdote is told of Whitney Hersh. Hersh was playing with Booth in Philadelphia at the time, and was well known for his ability to catch cold, a characteristic which won him many new friends but lost him several old ones. The theater where Booth was playing in *The Queen's Quandary, or What's Open Can't Be Shut,* was the old Chestnut Street Opera House which stood at the corner of what was then Arch, Chestnut, Spruce, Pine and Curly Maple Streets. This theater was noted in the profession for its slanting stage, so much so, in fact, that Booth, on hearing that they were to play there, is said to have remarked: "The Chestnut Street, eh?" On being assured that he had heard

UP AND AWAY

OR NOBODY KNOWS BUT NERO

OR THREE TIMES SIX IS EIGHTEEN

(Choice of any two titles)

Jonathan Henchman, father of Ralph Henchman and Mother of Men, Old Yale.......	MR. MACREADY
Ralph Henchman, father of Jonathan Henchman and a rather wild young chap....	MR. JUNIUS BOOTH
Jack Wyman, M.D., a doctor who has more "patience" than "patients".............	MR. EDMUND KEENE
Professor Hawksworth, an irascible old fellow who specializes in bird troubles.....	MR. HORNBLOW
Professor Hawksworth, an irascible old fellow who specializes in bird troubles.....	MR. JUNIUS BOOTH
Meeker, a party who lives by his wits and not much of that	MR. JONATHAN EDWARDS
Eugenia, daughter of Jonathan Henchman............	MRS. SIDDONS
Mlle. de Bon-Ton, a young lady who is not above drinking a little champagne now and then...................	MISS CUSHMAN
Eliza, maid at the Nortons...	BY HERSELF
Hamlet, Prince of Denmark..	MR. WILLIAM A. BRADY

correctly, Booth simply smiled. He later founded the Player's Club.

In *The Queen's Quandary, or What's Open Can't Be Shut,* Hersh had to play the part of *Rod-*

ney Ransome, the father of several people. In the second act there was a scene in which *Rodney* had to say to *Marian:*

"But I thought you said the Duke *had* no moustache!"

To which *Marian* was supposed to reply: "I never was more serious in all my life."

On the night of the opening performance Hersh was, as usual, very nervous. He got through the first act all right, with the aid of several promptings from his mother who was sitting in the balcony. But when the second act came along, it was evident to the other members of the company that Hersh could not be relied upon. This feeling was strengthened by the fact that he was nowhere to be found. They searched high and low for him but, like the sword of Damocles, he had disappeared. At the curtain to the second act, however, he was discovered sitting out front in D-113 applauding loudly and calling out: "Hersh! We-want-Hersh!" The only way they could get him back on the stage was a ruse which was not without its pathetic side. The manager of the house stepped out in front of the curtain and asked if any member of the audience would volunteer to come upon the stage and be hypnotized. Hersh, who had always wanted to go on the stage, was one of the first to push his way up. Once behind the footlights again his nervousness left him and he went on with his part where he had left off. It did not fit in with the rest of the play, but they were all so glad to have him back in the cast again that they said nothing about it to him, and whenever, in later years, he himself mentioned the affair, it was always as "that time in Philadelphia when I was so nervous." . . . And that little girl was Charlotte Cushman.

It was at this time that Stopford's *A New Way With Old Husbands, or The Mysterious Drummer-Boy,* was given its first performance at the old Garrick Theater in New York. The old Garrick Theater was torn down in 1878 to make way for the new Garrick Theater, which, in its turn, was torn down in 1880 to make way for the old Garrick again. It is the old, or new, Garrick which now stands at Broadway and Tenth Street on the spot known to passers-by as "Wanamaker's." Thus is the silver cord loosed and the pitcher broken at the well.

A New Way With Old Husbands, or The Mysterious Drummer-Boy was written for Ada Rehan, but she was in Fall River at the time; so the part was given to a young woman who had come to the theater that morning asking if a Mr. Wasserman lived there. On being told that it was not a private dwelling and that there was no one there named Wasserman, she had said.

"Well, then, does anyone here want to subscribe to the *Saturday Evening Post*?"

Those members of the cast who had gathered on the bare stage for rehearsal were so impressed by the young woman's courage that a purse was taken up for her children in case she had any and, in case she had no children, for her next of kin.

"I do not want money," she said, taking it. "All I want is a chance to prove my ability on the stage."

"Can you make the sound of crashing glass?" asked Arthur Reese, the stage manager.

"I think so," replied the young woman without looking up.

Reese looked at Meany, the assistant stage manager. "She is the one we want," he said quietly.

So the young woman was engaged. . . . Some thirty years later the Empire Theater in New York was aglow with lights on the occasion of the opening of *Call the Doctor*. Gay ladies, bejeweled and bejabbered, were running back and forth in the lobby, holding court, while tall, dark gentlemen in evening dress danced attendance. Those who couldn't dance sat it out. It was the metropolitan season at its height.

Suddenly a man burst excitedly through the crowd and made his way to the box-office.

"This seat is ridiculous," he exclaimed to the Treasurer of the theater (Roger M. Wakle, at the time). "I can't even see the stage from it."

"That is not so strange as it may seem to you at first," replied Wakle, "for the curtain is not up yet."

A hush fell over the crowded lobby. This was followed somewhat later by a buzz of excitement. This, in turn, was followed by a detail of mounted police. Men looked at women and at each other.

. . . For that young man was Charlotte Cushman.

It was about this time, as I remember it (or maybe later) that the old Augustin Daly Stock Company was at the top of its popularity and everyone was excited over the forthcoming production of *Up and Away*. It had been in rehearsal for several weeks when Tom Nevers asked Daly how much longer they were going to rehearse.

"Oh, about another week," replied Daly, with that old hat which later made him famous.

You can imagine Nevers' feelings!

A glance at the cast assembled for this production might be of interest in the light of subsequent events (the completion of the vehicular tunnel and the Centennial Exposition). So anyway it is in the middle of page 57 to look at if you want to.

As it turned out, *Up and Away* was never produced, as it was found to be too much trouble. But the old Augustin Daly Stock Company will not soon be forgotten.

My memories of St. Louis are of the pleasantest. We played there in Dante's *Really Mrs. Warrington*—and *Twelfth Night*. The *St. Louis Post-Dispatch*, on the morning following our opening, said:

"It is quite probable that before the end of the year we shall see the beginning of the end of the work on the McNaffen Dam. The project has been under construction now for three years and while there can be no suspicion thrown on the awarding

247

of the contracts, nevertheless we must say that the work has progressed but slowly."

It was while we were playing in St. Louis that the news came of the capture of J. Wilkes Booth. A performance of *Richelieu* was in progress, in which I was playing *Rafferty*, and Fanny Davenport the *Queen*. In the second act there is a scene in which *Rafferty* says to *La Pouce*:

> *"I can not, tho' my tongue were free,*
> *Repeat the message that my liege inspires,*
> *And tho' you ask it, were it mine,*
> *And hope you'll be my Valentine."*

Following this speech, *Rafferty* falls down and opens up a bad gash in his forehead.

We had come to this scene on the night I mention, when I noticed that the audience was tittering. I could not imagine what the matter was, and naturally thought of all kinds of things—sheep jumping over a fence—anything. But strange as it may seem, the tittering continued, and I have never found out, from that day to this what amused them so. . . . This was in 1878.

And now we come to the final curtain. For, after all, I sometimes think that Life is like a stage itself. The curtain rises on our little scene; we have our exits and our entrances, and each man in his time plays many parts. I must work this simile up sometime.

Life and the Theater. Who knows? *Selah*.

The Low State
of Whippet Racing

IT DOES not seem too soon now to begin formulating plans for next year's whippet racing. While there are still a few more races on the 1928 schedule, most of the important ones have been run off and the leading whippets have practically all broken training.

Whippet racing in recent years has deteriorated into a sordid spectacle, productive only of gigantic gate receipts for the promoters. At one whippet race on Long Island last summer, it is estimated that forty people lined the course, and, as each of these forty paid something in the neighborhood of a quarter for parking their cars in a nearby field, it will be seen that the thing has already got out of hand and is now in the class of mad sport carnivals.

This has naturally had its reaction on the whippets themselves. They have become mercenary and callous. All they think of is money, money, money. The idea of sport for sport's sake is a dream of the past as far as whippets are concerned. In order to make the game what it used to be, we shall have to bring up a whole new breed of whippets and send the present success-crazed organization out on the road in circuses where they may indulge their lust for gain without hindrance of any considerations of sportsmanship.

Perhaps a few examples may serve to illustrate my point. I witnessed a whippet race in California recently at which the gate happened to be very small. There had been no publicity worthy of the name and the word had simply got around among the racetrack gang that some whippets were going to race at three o'clock. This brought out a crowd of perhaps six people, exclusive of the owners and trainers. Four of the six were chance passers-by and the other two were state policemen.

Now evidently the small size of the crowd enraged the whippets or, at any rate, threw them into such a state of mind that they gave up all idea of racing and took to kidding. In the first race they were not halfway down the lanes when two of them stopped and walked back, while the other two began wrestling good-naturedly. The owners at the finish line called frantically, but to no avail, and the race had to be called off.

In the second race they would not even start. When the gun was fired, they turned as if by pre-arranged mutiny and began jumping up and kissing their trainers. This race also had to be called off.

By this time the crowd was in an ugly humor and one or two started to boo. The state police, scenting trouble, went home. This left four spectators and further upset the whippets. A conference of the owners and trainers resulted in what you might call practically nothing. It got along toward supper time and even I went home. I looked in the papers

By this time the crowd was in an ugly humor

the next morning but could find no news of the races, so I gathered that the rest of the heats had been called off too.

This pretty well indicates the state in which whippet racing now finds itself in this country. The remedy is up to those of us old whippet fanciers who have the time and the means to reform the thing from the ground up.

First, I would recommend a revision of the system of whippet-calling. As you no doubt know, a whippet race is at least one-third dependent on calling. The trainer leads the whippet from the finish line up the lane to the starting point (a silly procedure to begin with) and then holds him in leash until the gun. The owner, or some close personal friend, stands at the finish line and calls to the whippet, which is supposed to drive him crazy and make him run like mad back down the lane again in a desire to reach his owner. As we have seen, the whippet can take it or leave it and is by no means certain to show any desire at all to get back to the caller. Now this must be due to the calling. If the thing were made attractive at all for the whippet to reach the finish line, we would see no more of this hopping up and kissing trainers at the start.

As near as I could distinguish, most of the owners called out, "Come on, Luke!" or "Here, Bennie, here!" Now obviously there was nothing very exciting about these calls. You or I wouldn't run like mad down a lane to get to someone who was calling, "Come on, Charlie!" or "Here, Bob, here!" (unless, of course, it was Greta Garbo who was doing the calling. In that case, a short, sharp whistle would be O.K.).

There must be some more attractive sounds made to entice the whippets down the lanes. Not knowing exactly what it is that whippets like best, it is a little difficult for me to make suggestions. I don't know and I don't pretend to know. All I am sure of is that the whippets aren't particularly attracted by what is being held out to them now.

Now in the matter of blankets. On the way up the lanes to the starting point, the whippets are forced to wear blankets like race horses. This saps not only their vitality but their self-respect. It is all right for a race horse to wear a blanket if he wants to, because he is big and can carry it off well. But when you get a whippet who, even with everything showing, can hardly be seen unless you have him in your lap, and then cover him up in a blanket, it just makes a nance out of him, that's all. They look like so many trotting blankets, and they must know it. A whippet has feelings as well as the rest of us. You can't make a dog ashamed to appear in public and then expect him to run a race. If they have to be kept warm, give each one a man's-size shot of rye before he starts up the course. You'd get better racing that way, too. With a good hooker of rye inside him, a whippet might not really be running fast but he would think that he was, and that's something. As it stands, they are so ashamed

It just makes a nance out of him

of their blankets that they have to do something on the way down the lanes to appear virile. So they stop right in the middle of the race and wrestle.

This wrestling business calls for attention, too. It is all right for dogs to kid, but they don't have to do it in the middle of a race. It is as if Charlie Paddock, while running the hundred, should stop after about fifty yards and push one of his opponents playfully on the shoulder and say, "Last tag!" and then as if his opponent should stop and chase Charlie around in the track trying to tag him back. What kind of time would they make in a race like that?

I don't think that the thing has ever been put up to the whippets quite frankly in this manner.

The owner or some close personal friend stands at the finish line and calls to the whippet

If someone could take a few whippets to a track meet and (the whole gag having been worked up before, of course, among the runners) the thing should deteriorate into a rough-and-tumble clowning match of pushing and hauling one another, the whippets might see what it looks like. You could say to them: "Now you see, that's how *you* look when you stop in the middle of a race and wrestle all over the track." They would be pretty ashamed, I should think.

The less said about their jumping up and kissing their trainers at the start, the better. This is something that a good psychoanalyst ought to

256

handle. But so long as it is allowed to go on, whippet racing will be in the doldrums. And so long as whippet racing is in the doldrums—well, it is in the doldrums, that's all.

Better in the doldrums, say I, than for the whippets to so far forget the principles of good, clean amateur sport as to pursue a mechanical rabbit.

The Cooper Cycle
in American Folk Songs

A STUDY of the folk-songs of—and indigenous to—the Ohio River Valley (and just a teeny-weeny section of Illinois) discloses the fact that, between 1840 and half-past nine, coopering was the heroic occupation and coopers the legendary heroes of local song and story.

On all sides we come across fragments of ballads, or even the ballads themselves, dealing with the romantic deeds of such characters as *Cris the Cooper*, or *Warburton the Barrel-Maker*, with an occasional reference to *William W. Ransome*, although there is no record of *Ransome's* having been a cooper.

The style in which these cooper-ballads were written would indicate that they were all written by members of the same family, possibly the Jukes. There is the same curious, stilted rhyme-scheme, more like a random idea than a scheme, and a mannerism of harmony which indicates clearly that they were composed on a comb.

Probably the most famous of all these ballads in praise of coopering is the one called "Ernie Henkle," which begins as follows:

"Oh, my name is Ernie Henkle,
    Oh, in Rister I was born,
    Oh, I never let up with my coopering
    Oh, till I get my rintle on."

(A rintle was the special kind of thumb-piece
that coopers used to thumb down the hoops, before
the invention of the automatic hooper.)

"Oh, one day 'twas down in Georgia,
    And that I won't deny,
    That I met a gal named Sadie Fried,
    And—(*line lost*)

"Oh, she stole my heart completely,
    And that I can't deny,
    And it wasn't the tenth of August
    Or the eighteenth of July."

(Here the singer interjects a whistling solo.)

"When up stepped Theodore Munson,
    And unto me did say,
    'Oh, you can't go back on your promised word,'
    And unto me did say.

"Oh, I killed that Theodore Munson,
    And unto him did say,
    'Oh, the only gal is Henrietta Bascome,
    And that you can't deny.'"

This goes on for thirty-seven verses and then begins over again and goes over the entire thirty-

seven for the second time. By this time every one is pretty sick of it.

But there we see the cooper-ballad at its best. (If you don't believe it, you ought to hear some of the others.) *Ernie Henkle* came to stand for the heroic cooper and, even in later songs about baggage-men, we find the *Henkle* motif creeping in—and out again.

For example, in the famous song about "Joe McGee, the Baggage-Man":

> " 'Twas in the gay December,
>   And the snow was up to your knees,
> When Number 34 pulled 'round the bend
>   As pretty as you please.
> Lord, Lord. As pretty as you please.
>
> "Now Joe McGee was the baggage-man,
>   On Number 34,
> And he sat right down on the engine step
>   And killed that Sam Basinette."

(There seems to be some confusion here as to just *what* Sam Basinette is meant. He must have been referred to in an earlier verse which has been lost.)

> "Now Sam Basinette said before he died,
>   'This ain't no treat to me,
> For the only gal is Henrietta Bascome,
>   And that you will agree.' "

It seems that *Henrietta Bascome* was more or less

of a prom-girl who rotated between the coopers and the baggage-men in their social affairs, and even got as far north as Minnesota when the roads were clear.

It will be seen that in all these folk-songs the picaresque element is almost entirely lacking: that is, there is very little—perhaps I mean "picturesque" instead of "picaresque." In all these songs the *picturesque* element is lacking; that is, there is very little color, very little movement, very little gin, please. The natives of this district were mostly rude people—constantly bumping into each other and never apologizing—and it is quite likely that they thought these to be pretty good songs, as songs go. That they aren't, is no fault of mine. You ought to know better than to read an article on American folk-songs.

Fascinating Crimes

5. The Strange Case of the Vermont Judiciary

RESIDENTS of Water Street, Bellows Falls (Vt.), are not naturally sound sleepers, owing to the proximity of the Bellows Falls Light and Power Co. and its attendant thumpings, but fifteen years before the erection of the light-and-power plant there was nothing to disturb the slumbers of Water Streetites, with the possible exception of the bestial activities of Roscoe Erkle. For it was Mr. Erkle's whim to creep up upon people as they slept and, leaping on their chests, to cram poisoned biscuits into their mouths until they died, either from the poison or from choking on the crumbs.

A tolerant citizenry stood this as long as it could decently be expected to, and then had Roscoe Erkle arrested. It is not this phase of his career in which we are interested, however, so much as the remarkable series of events which followed.

His trial began at St. Albans, Franklin County, on Wednesday morning, May 7, 1881. Defending Erkle was an attorney appointed by the Court, Enos J. Wheefer. Mr. Wheefer, being deaf, had not heard the name of his client or he would never have taken the case. He thought for several days that he was defending Roscoe Conkling and had drawn up his case with Conkling in mind.

Atty. Herbert J. McNell represented the State

and, as it later turned out, a tragic fate gave the case into the hands of Judge Alonso Presty for hearing.

Judge Presty was one of the leaders of the Vermont bar at the time and a man of impeccable habits. It was recalled after his untimely death that he had been something of a rounder in his day, having been a leader in barn-dancing circles while in law school, but since donning the sock and buskin his conduct had been propriety itself. Which make the events that we are about to relate all the more puzzling.

On the opening day of the trial, Atty. McNell was submitting as evidence passages from the prisoner's diary which indicated that the murders were not only premeditated but a source of considerable delight to Mr. Erkle. It might perhaps be interesting to give a sample page from the diary:

"*Oct.* 7—Cool and fair. Sharp tinge of Fall in the air. New shipment of arsenic arrived from W. Spent all day powdering biscuits and then toasting them. Look good enough to eat.

"*Oct.* 8—Raw, with N. E. wind. Betsy came in for a minute and we did anagrams. (EDITOR'S NOTE: *Betsy was Erkle's cow.*)

"*Oct.* 9—Still raw. Cleaned up Water Street on the left-hand side, with the exception of old Wassner who just wouldn't open his mouth. Home and read till after midnight. That man Carlyle certainly had the dope on the French Revolution, all right, all right."

As Atty. McNell read these excerpts from the diary in a droning voice, the breath of Vermont May-time wafted in at the open windows of the courtroom. Now and then a bee hummed in and out, as if to say: "Buz-z-z-z-z-z-z!" Judge Presty sat high above the throng, head resting on his hand, to all intents and purposes asleep.

Suddenly the attorney for the defendant arose and said: "I protest, Your Honor. I cannot hear what my learned colleague is saying, but I don't like his expression!"

There was silence while all eyes turned on the Judge. But the Judge did not move. Thinking that he had fallen asleep, as was his custom during the May term, the attorneys went on. It was not until he had gradually slipped forward into the glass of water which stood before him on his desk that it was discovered that he was dead!

The trial was immediately halted and an investigation begun. Nothing could be discovered about the Judge's person which would give a clue to his mysterious lapse except a tiny red spot just behind his right ear. This, however, was laid to indigestion and the Judge was buried.

Another trial was called for October 10, again in St. Albans. This time Judge Walter M. Bondy was presiding, and the same two attorneys opposed each other. Roscoe Erkle had, during the summer, raised a red beard and looked charming.

On the second day of the trial, while Atty. McNell was reading the prisoner's diary, Judge Bondy passed away quietly at his bench, with the same little red spot behind his right ear that had characterized the cadaver of his predecessor. The trial was again halted, and a new one set for the following May.

By this time, the matter had become one for serious concern. Erkle was questioned, but his only reply was: "Let them mind their own business, then." He had now begun to put pomade on his beard and had it parted in the middle, and, as a result, had married one of the richest spinsters in that section of Vermont.

We need not go into the repetitious account of the succeeding trials. Suffice it to say that the following May Judge Rapf died at his post, the following October Judge Orsenigal, the May following that a Judge O'Heel, who had been imported from New Hampshire without being told the history of the case, and the succeeding solstices saw the mysterious deaths of Judges Wheefer (the counsel for the defense in the first trial, who had, in the meantime, been appointed Judge because of his deafness), Rossberg, Whelan, Rock, and Brady. And, in each case, the little telltale mark behind the ear.

The State then decided to rest its case and declare it *nol-prossed*. Judges were not so plentiful in Vermont that they could afford to go on at this rate. Erkle was released on his own recognizance, took up the study of law, and is, at latest accounts, a well-to-do patent attorney in Oldham. Every May and every October he reports at St. Albans to see if they want to try him again, but the Court laughingly postpones the case until the next term, holding its hand over its right ear the while.

The Passing of
the Cow

*(With Wild West Sketches from the Author's
Notebook)*

ONE of the signs of the gradual deterioration
of the West is the even more gradual disappearance of the cow. By "cow" is meant any heavy
animal that lumbers along mooing, regardless of
sex. There has been too much attention paid to
sex lately.

According to the startling statistics of the U. S.
Cow-Counting Bureau issued on Monday (for release Wednesday), there are not more than six or
seven real cows left in the West. This, at first
blush, would seem to be an understatement when
one thinks of the number of animals that *look* like
cows that one sees from the back of the prairie-
schooner as one drives across the plains. But certainly the U. S. Cow-Counting Bureau ought to
know a cow when it sees one. These other animals
must be impostors.

Accepting these statistics—or this statistic—as
genuine, we find ourselves confronted by a pretty
serious situation. The cow has been called "Man's
best friend." No, that is the dog. . . . Sorry.

The situation is serious, regardless of who Man's

best friend is. Without cows (and if, when these figures were compiled, there were only six or seven

Horse and rider

(If I were doing this over again, I would put a large cactus in to hide the horse's front legs. And maybe his hind ones, too. Perhaps I would just have the cowboy standing there.)

left in the West, it is safe to assume that even these are gone by now) things look pretty black. It sometimes seems as if it were hardly worth while going on.

Ever since 1847 the cow has been the feature of the West that most appealed to the imagination. Prior to 1847 it was thought that all these animals were horses. You can imagine the surprise of the man who first discovered otherwise.

With the discovery of cows came the cowboy.

One of the steers that has disappeared
(*This is easily the worst drawing of the lot. It has, however, caught something of the spirit of the old West.*)

And with the cowboy came the moving picture. So you see!

It is related, in an old cowboy ballad, how the first cow was lassoed. It seems that Ernest Guilfoil, known as "Mr. Ernest Guilfoil," was practicing swinging his rope one day, trying to synchronize gum-chewing with rope-twirling so that he could work in a monologue between the two and go on the stage. He had the gum-chewing and monologue all synchronized, but was having trouble with the rope. Suddenly, after a particularly complicated session with the "pesky" thing, he felt a tug on the other end and, on reeling it in, discovered that he had entangled a cow in the noose. Terrified, he jumped on his pony and rode to the nearest corral, dragging the luckless cow behind him. Thus "Mr. Ernest Guilfoil" became the first cowboy.

The first inkling that the world at large had of

269

Cowboy chasing cow

(It has never been very easy for me to draw animals, and it seems to be getting harder and harder as I grow older. For instance, that cow is not right and I know it. The horse is a little better, but seems to have too much personality. At any rate, the etching has action. Perhaps it would have been better to write an article just about cowboys themselves.)

the lack of cows was the concentration of cowboys in rodeos and Wild West shows. Here it was possible for a dozen or so cowboys to work on one cow, using the same one over and over at each performance. But it was not until the Bureau of Cow-Counting made its staggering analysis that the public finally realized what had happened. And now it is too late. Just what is to be done about it is a problem. Some suggest moving a lot of cows on from the East, but old-time Westerners feel that this would be adding insult to injury. The alternative seems to be to bring the cowboys on to where the cows are, but that wouldn't work out either, because—oh, because it *wouldn't,* that's all.

And so it comes about that romance dies and Civilization charges ahead. But some of us are wondering, "Is it all worth it?"

A Short (What There Is of It) History of American Political Problems

CHAP. I VOL. I.

IN OUR two introductions to this history (one of which was lost) we made a general survey of the development of political theory and practice from Plato down to Old Man ("He Must Know Nothin' ") River. In beginning our history proper, it might perhaps be wise to forget all that we have said before and start fresh, as a lot of new things have come up since the last introduction was written (such as the Abolition of Slavery and the entire Reconstruction Period) which have changed the political aspect considerably.

We will begin our history, therefore, with the year 1800; in the first place, because 1800 is a good round number and easily remembered (Vanderbilt 1800, for instance), and in the second place, because it marked the defeat of the Federalist Party under Hamilton by the Republicans under Jefferson.

Now you are going to start back in astonishment when I say "Republicans under Jefferson" and most likely will write in and say, "What do you mean, *Republicans* under Jefferson, you big old gump you! Everybody knows that it was Jefferson who founded the *Democratic* Party. . . . Yours truly (whatever your name happens to be). . . ."

And here is where I will have the laugh on you, because you will have forgotten what I told you in one of our introductions to this history about the present Democratic Party having once been called the Republican Party. So when I say "Republicans under Jefferson" I *mean* "Republicans under Jefferson" and no more back talk out of you, either. If you had devoted half the time to reading one, or both, of the introductions to this history that you devote to jazz and petting-parties you would know something about the political history of your country instead of being such a nimcompoop. (There was a political party named the "Nimcompoops" a little later on, and I can hardly wait to tell you about it. . . . Perhaps I won't wait. I may tell about it any minute now. [ADV.])

Now the reason for the defeat of the Federalists in 1800 was based on several influences which have a rather important bearing on our story. They were:

1. The Federalists (as I have told you again and again until I am sick of it) thought that the Federal Government ought to have the power to rule the various states with a rod of iron. A good way to remember this by means of an old rhyme: "The Federalists thought that the Federal Government ought to have the power to rule the various states with a rod of iron. Rum-tiddy-um-tum-tum-tiron!"

272

2. Hamilton himself was very snooty.

3. Adams (John), the Federalist President, was very snooty and a Harvard man into the bargain.

4. No one ever had any fun.

Jefferson, on the other hand, believed that the various states ought to be allowed to govern themselves, using the Federal Government only when company came or when there was a big reception or something. This appealed to the various states, and as, after all, the various states were made up of the voters themselves and the Federal Government consisted chiefly of Hamilton and Adams and their families, it is little wonder that, on a majority vote, the various states won.

So, in 1801, Thomas Jefferson took over the reins of the government and the Republican Party had its first opportunity to show the strength of its principles.

But we are getting ahead of our story.

In our next chapter we will take up the final collapse of the Federalists and the appearance of the Whigs.

Back
to the Game

THIS is about the time of year (it would be a good joke on me if this chapter were held over until Spring) when the old boys begin thinking of going back to college to the Big Game. All during the year they have never given a thought to whether they were alumni of Yale or the New York Pharmaceutical College, but as soon as the sporting pages begin telling about O'Brienstein of Harvard and what a wonderful back he is, all Harvard men with cigar-ashes on their waistcoats suddenly remember that they went to Harvard and send in their applications for the Yale Game. There is nothing like a college education to broaden a man.

Going back to the old college town is something of an ordeal, in case you want to know. You think it's going to be all right and you have a little dream-picture of how glad the boys will be to see you. "Weekins, 1914" you will say, and there will be a big demonstration, with fire-works and retchings. The word will go round that Weekins, 1914, is back and professors in everything but Greek will say to their classes: "Dismissed for the day, gentlemen. Weekins, 1914, is back!" And a happy crowd of boys will rush pell-mell out of the recitation-hall and down to the Inn to take the horses from your carriage (or put horses into it) and drag you all around the Campus. (My using the word "Campus" is just a concession to the rabble. Where I come from "Campus" is a place where stage-collegians in skull-caps romp around and sing "When Love Is Young in Springtime" in four-part harmony. The reservation in question is known as "the Yard," and I will thank you to call it that in future.)

Anyone who has ever gone back to the old college town after, let us say, ten years, will realize that this country is going to the dogs, especially as regards its youth in the colleges. You get your tickets for the Big Game and you spend a lot of money on railroad fare. (That's all right; you have made a lot of money since getting out. You can afford it.) When you get to the old railroad station you can at least expect that Eddie, the hack-driver, will remember you. Eddie, however, is now pretty fat and has five men working for him. You can't even get one of his cabs, much less a nod out of him. "O. K. Eddie! The hell with you!"

You go to the fraternity house (another concession on my part to my Middle West readers) and announce yourself as "Weekins, 1914." (My class was 1912, as a matter of fact. I am giving myself a slight break and trying to be mysterious about this whole thing.) A lone Junior who is hanging around in the front room says "How do you do? Come on in," and excuses himself immediately.

The old place looks about the same, except that an odd-looking banner on the wall says "1930," there being no such year. A couple of young men come in and, seeing you, go right out again. Welcome back to the old House, Weekins!

A couple of young men come in and, seeing you, go right out again

A steward of some sort enters the room and arranges the magazines on the table.

"Rather quiet for the day of the Big Game," you say to him. "Where is everybody?"

276

This frightens him and he says: "Thank you, sir!" and also disappears.

Well, after all, you *do* have a certain claim on this place. You helped raise the money for the mission furniture and somewhere up on the wall is a stein with your name on it. There is no reason why you should feel like an intruder. This gives you courage to meet the three young men who enter with books under their arms and pass right by into the hall.

"My name is Weekins, 1914," you say. "Where is everybody?"

"Classes are just over," one of them explains. "Make yourself at home. My name is Hammerbiddle, 1931."

Somehow the mention of such a year as "1931" enrages you. "1931 what? Electrons?" But the three young men have gone down the hall; so you will never know.

A familiar face! In between the bead portières comes a man, bald and fat, yet with something about him that strikes an old G chord.

"Billigs!" you cry.

"Stanpfer is the name," he says. "Think of seeing you here!"

You try to make believe that you knew that it was Stanpfer all the time and were just saying Billigs to be funny.

"It must be fifteen years," you say.

"Well, not quite," says Stanpfer, "I saw you two years ago in New York."

"Oh, yes, I know, *that!*" (Where the hell did you see him two years ago? The man is crazy.) "But I mean it must be fifteen years since we were here together."

"Fourteen," he corrects.

"I guess you're right. Fourteen. Well, how the hell are you?"

"Great! How are you?"

"Great! How are you?"

"Great! Couldn't be better. Everything going all right?"

"Great! All right with you?"

"Great! All right with you?"

"You bet."

"That's fine! Kind of quiet around here."

"That's right! Not much like the old days."

"That's right."

"Yes, sir! That's right!"

Perhaps it would be better if the 1931 boys came back. At least, you wouldn't have to recall old days with them. You could start at scratch. Here comes somebody! Somebody older than you, if such a thing is possible.

"Hello," he says, and falls on his face against the edge of the table, cutting his forehead rather badly.

"Up you get!" you say, suiting the action to the word.

"A very nasty turn there," he says, crossly. "They should have that banked."

"That's right," you agree. You remember him as

278

a Senior who was particularly snooty to you when you were a sophomore.

"My name is Feemer, 1911," he says, dabbing his forehead with his handkerchief.

"Weekins, 1914," you say.

"Stanpfer, 1914," says Billigs.

"I remember you," says Feemer, "you were an awful pratt."

You give a short laugh.

Feemer begins to sing loudly and hits his head again against the table, this time on purpose. Several of the undergraduates enter and look disapprovingly at all three of you.

By this time Feemer, through constant hitting of his head and lurching about, is slightly ill. The general impression is that you and Stanpfer (or Billigs) are drunk too. These old grads!

The undergraduates (of whom there are now eight or ten) move unpleasantly about the room, rearranging furniture that Feemer has upset and showing in every way at their disposal that they wish you had never come.

"What time is the game?" you ask. You know very well what time the game is.

Nobody answers.

"How are the chances?" Just why you should be making *all* the advances you don't know. After all, you are fourteen years out and these boys could almost be your sons.

"I want everybody here to come to Chicago with me after the game," says Feemer, tying his tie. "I live in Chicago and I want everybody here to come to Chicago with me after the game. I live in Chicago and I want everybody here to come to Chicago with me after the game."

Having made this blanket invitation, Feemer goes to sleep standing up.

The undergraduate disapproval is manifest and includes you and Billigs (or Stanpfer) to such an extent that you might better be at the bottom of the lake.

"How are the chances?" you ask again. "Is Derkwillig going to play?"

"Derkwillig has left college," says one of the undergraduates, scornfully. "He hasn't played since the Penn State game."

"Too bad," you say. "He was good, wasn't he?"

"Not so good."

"I'm sorry. I thought he was, from what I read in the papers."

"The papers are crazy," says a very young man, and immediately leaves the room.

There is a long silence, during which Feemer comes to and looks anxiously into each face as if trying to get his bearings, which is exactly what he is trying to do.

"We might as well clear the room out," says one of the undergraduates. "The girls will be coming pretty soon and we don't want to have it looking messy."

Evidently "looking messy" means the presence of you, Feemer and Stanpfer. This is plain to be

There is no sign of recognition on either side

seen. So you and Stanpfer each take an arm of Feemer and leave the house. Just as you are going down the steps (a process which includes lurching with Feemer from side to side) you meet Dr. Raddiwell and his wife. There is no sign of recognition on either side.

There is a train leaving town at 1:55. You get it and read about the game in the evening papers.

The Four-in-Hand
Outrage

WHAT has happened to four-in-hand ties that they refuse to slide around under the collar any more? Or am I just suffering from a persecution complex?

For maybe ten years I have been devoted to the soft collar or sport model, the polo shirt, and other informal modes in collarings affected by the *jeunesse dorée*. They have not been particularly adapted to playing up my good points in personal appearance, but they are easy to slip into in the morning.

With the approach of portly middle-age, however, and the gradual but relentless assumption of power in the financial world, it seemed to me that I ought to dress the part. When a man goes into a bank to ask to have his note extended he should at least wear a stiff collar and a four-in-hand of some rich, dark material, preferably a foulard. He owes it to himself.

So I laid in a stock of shirts (two) which called for either stiff collars or a knotted bandana, and then set about digging up some collars to go with them. My old stock of "Graywoods 14½" which I used to wear in high-school proved useless. They were of the mode, so flashy in those days, which

*I have been devoted to informal modes of **Collarings**
affected by the* jeunesse dorée

came close together in front, allowing just a tip of the knitted club-tie to peek out from under the corners. And, owing to a temporary increase in neck-size (I can reduce it at any time by dieting for two or three days), 14½ is no longer my number. So I bought several styles of a more modern collar and prepared to throw the world of fashion into a tumult by appearing in formal neckwear on, let us say, the following Wednesday at high noon.

But in the ten years which have elapsed since I last tied a four-in-hand under a stiff collar something perverse has been injected into the manufacture of either the ties or the collars. My male readers will recognize a manœuvre which I can best designate as the Final Tug, the last short pull-around of the tie under the collar before tightening the knot. This, under the present system, has become practically impossible. The tie refuses to budge; I pull and yank, take the collar off and re-arrange the tie, try gentle tactics, followed suddenly by a deceptive upward jerk, but this gets me nothing. The knot stays loosely off-center and the tie appears to be stuck somewhere underneath the collar at a point perhaps three inches to the right. After two minutes of this mad wrenching one of three things happens—the tie rips, the collars tears, or I strangle to death in a horrid manner with eyes bulging and temples distended, a ghastly caricature of my real self.

Now this is a very strange thing to have happened in ten years. It can't be that I have forgotten how.

The tie refuses to budge

It can't be that I have lost that amount of strength through loose living. It must be that some deliberate process has been adopted by the manufacturers to prevent four-in-hands from slipping under collars. What their idea can be is a mystery. You'd think they would *want* to make things as easy for their patrons as possible. But no! Modern business *efficiency*, I suppose! The manufacturers were

288

in conference, I suppose! Rest-rooms for their women employees . . . oh, yes! Time clocks, charts, paper drinking-cups . . . oh, yes! But collars that hold ties immovable, and ties that stick in collars. That's what *we* get. That's what the Public gets. Prohibition was foisted on our boys while they were overseas, and while I was wearing soft collars the Powers-That-Be were putting the devil into stiff ones, so that when I come back to wearing them again I strangle myself to death. A fine civilization, I must say!

A Christmas Garland
of Books

AMONG the little bundle of books especially selected for Christmas-Wistmas, perhaps the most pat is "Rubber Hand Stamps and the Manipulation of India Rubber" by T. O'Conor Sloane. Into it Mr. Sloane has put the spirit of Yuletide which all of us must feel, whether we are cynical enough to deny it or not.

Beginning with a short, and very dirty, history of the sources of India Rubber, the author takes us by the hand and leads us into the fairy-land of rubber manipulation. And it is well that he does, for without his guidance we should have made an awful mess of the next rubber-stamp we tried to make. As he says on page 35: "It will be evident from the description to come that it is not advisable for anyone without considerable apparatus to attempt to clean and wash ("to sheet"), to masticate, or to mix india rubber." Even if we had the apparatus, we would probably be content with simply "sheeting" and mixing the india rubber and leave the masticating for other less pernickety people to go through with. We may be an old maid about such things, but it is too late now for us to learn to like new things.

It seems that in the making of rubber stamps a

preparation known as "flong" is necessary. Mr. Sloane assures us that anyone who has watched the stereotyping of a large daily newspaper knows what "flong" is. Perhaps our ignorance is due to the fact that we were on the editorial end of a daily newspaper and went down into the composing-room only when it was necessary to rescue some mistake we had made from the forms. At any rate, we didn't know what "flong" was and we don't want to know. A man must keep certain reticences these days or he will just have no standards left at all.

It is not generally known how simple it is to make things out of rubber. "The writer has obtained excellent results from pieces of an old discarded bicycle tire. The great point is to apply a heavy pressure to the hot material. Many other articles can be thus produced extemporaneously." (Page 78.) This should lend quite a bit of excitement to the manipulation of india rubber. Imagine working along quietly making, let us say, rubber type and then finding that, extemporaneously, you had a rubber Negro doll or balloon on your hands! A man's whole life could be changed by such a fortuitous slip of the rubber.

Not the least of Mr. Sloane's contributions to popular knowledge is his sly insertion, under the very noses of the authorities, of what he calls the "Old Home Receipt" (ostensibly for "roller-composition," but we know better, eh, Mr. Sloane?). The "Old Home Receipt" specifies "Glue 2 lbs. soaked over night, to New Orleans molasses 1

gallon. Not durable, but excellent while it lasts."
We feel sure that we have been served something
made from this "Old Home Receipt," but would
suggest to Mr. Sloane that he try putting in just a
dash of absinthe. It makes it more durable.

We can recommend Laurence Vail Coleman's
"Manual for Small Museums" to all those who have
received or are about to give small museums for
Christmas. Having a small museum on your hands
with no manual for it is no joke. It sometimes seems
as if a small museum were more bother than a large
one, but that is only when one is tired and cross.

From Mr. Coleman's remarkably comprehensive
study of small museums, we find that, as is so often
the case, income is a very serious problem. In
financing special projects for the museum, such as
the purchase of bird groups (if it is a museum that
wants bird groups), there is a great play for in-
genuity, and Dr. Abbott of the San Diego Museum
of Natural History, tells of how they, in San Diego,
met the problem:

The little cases containing bird-groups were
offered to tradespeople in the city for display in
their windows, the understanding being that the
store should pay $50 for the advertising value.
Thus, a meadowlark group, representing the male
in very bright dress, the female, the nest and eggs,
was paid for by a men's and women's clothing store
and displayed in its window in the early spring with
the slogan: "Take a pointer from the birds. Now
is the time for your new spring clothes." A savings-

bank took a woodpecker group, showing the storing away of acorns, and a California shrike group (Dr. Abbott ought to know) showing a rather sanguinary example of impaling surplus prey on the spines of a cactus, both displayed under the euphemistic caption "The Saving Instinct" and "Are You Providing for the Future by storing up your dollars [or cadavers] now?" A bush-tit's nest was taken by a real-estate firm and a mockingbird group by a music house. The local lodge of Elks gave $1200 for a case holding four elks (not members) and so, in time, the entire housing of the groups was accomplished and paid for. We are crazy to know what business houses paid for the rabbit and owl exhibits.

In the chapter on "Protection from Pests" we looked for a way of dealing with the man in an alpaca coat who grabs your stick away from you as you enter the museum and the young people who use museums for necking assignations, but they were not specified. A blanket formula is given, however, which ought to cover their cases. "The surest way to get rid of pests is to fumigate with hydrocyanic acid in an airtight compartment, but this is a dangerous procedure which has resulted in a loss of human life. [Why "but"?] Another fumigant that is widely used is carbon bisulphide, but this is highly explosive and has caused serious accidents." This presents a new problem to museum-visitors and would seem to make the thing one of the major risks of modern civilization. If a person can't be safe from asphyxiation and mutilation

293

while looking at bird-groups, where *is* one to be safe? It would almost be better to let the pests go for a while, at least until the museum gets started.

A collection of verse entitled "Through the Years with Mother," compiled by Eva M. Young, makes a nice gift which might perhaps be given to Father. It contains most of the little poems which have been written about mothers and the general tone of the thing is favorable to motherhood. One, entitled "A Bit O' Joy," wears off a little into child-propaganda, but probably would rank as a mother-poem too, for it is presumably the mother who speaks:

> Just a Bit-a-Feller,
> Lips a bit o' rose,
> Puckered sort o' puzzled like,
> Wonder if he knows—

There is one more verse explaining what the Bit-a-Feller might possibly know, but we didn't go into that. Another one which we left for reading on the train was entitled: "Muvvers" and begins:

> One time, I wuz so very small,
> I prit' near wuzn't there at all—

We can not even tell you what the first two lines are of "Mama's Dirl."

The introduction to "Are Mediums Really Witches?" by John P. Touey begins by saying: "The sole purpose of this book, as its title suggests, is to prove the existence of a personal evil force and

294

demon intervention in human affairs." This frightened us right at the start, for we are very susceptible to any argument which presupposes a tough break for ourself. There must be *some* explanation for what happens to us every time we stick our head out doors—or in doors, for that matter.

Mr. Touey begins with witchcraft in ancient times and comes right straight down to the present day. Even though he quoted "no less an authority than Porphyrius" in his earlier chapter, it was not until we got into the examples of modern people having their bed-clothes pulled off and their hats thrown at them that we began to feel uneasy. The story of the terrible time had by the Fox Sisters in Hydesville, N. Y., seemed pretty conclusive to us at the time of reading (2:15 A.M. this morning) and, frankly, we stopped there. And, believe it or not, a couple of hours later, during our troubled sleep, *some*thing pulled the bed-clothes out from the foot of *our* bed, and we awoke with a nasty head-cold.

We will pay $100 to Mr. Touey or Sir Oliver Lodge or anyone else who can help us locate the personal demon who has been assigned to us. We would just like to talk to him for five minutes, the big bully!

We can quote but one example of the fascinating problems presented in John A. Zangerle's "Principles of Real Estate Appraising" as we are limited in our space assignment, but perhaps from it the reader may get some idea of the charm of the book:

"Mr. Flanagan of New Zealand values this interest on the basis of an annuity using the 5% interest tables. Calculating the value on a 6% basis he would proceed as follows: Lessor receives $6,000 per annum for ten years, the present value of which is 6,000 x 7.36 equals $44,160; plus the present value of $12,000 per annum for 89 years commencing ten years hence which is 12,000 x 9.254 (16.614—7.36) equals $111,048. Lessor is also entitled to receive either possession or rent after 99 years have expired, the reversionary value of which can be taken at $12,000 x 16.667 less 16.614 or .053 equals $636. Thus $11,048 plus $44,160 equals $155,844, the value of the lessor's interest."

How do you mean 16.614, Mr. Flanagan? Aren't you forgetting depreciation?

For those who like to browse along lazily with British royalty, we can think of no less charming way than to accompany Helen, Countess-Dowager of Radnor through her 361-page book: "From a Great-Grandmother's Armchair." We had almost decided not to begin it at all, until we read in the Countess-Dowager's preface: "At the present time I am resting 'on my oars' (or rather, in my Armchair) at my quiet country home, which, amongst those of the third generation, goes by the name of 'Grannie's Peace-pool.'" This gave us incentive to read further.

And what a treat! "Grannie" certainly has earned her "peace-pool" after the exciting life she has led. Every year of her long career is given here in detail and it must make fascinating reading for the Radnors if only as a record of where the Countess left her umbrella that time in Godalming and who played zither in her "Ladies' String Band and Chorus" in 1879.

Among other things that are cleared up in this volume is the question of what the Countess did during those first hectic weeks of July, 1901.

"A good many engagements were crowded into the first fortnight of July," she writes modestly, "before going back to Venice. Among other things I passed a very pleasant week-end at Wendover Lodge with Alfred and Lizzie Gatty."

But the book does not dwell entirely in the past. Right up to the present day we have disclosures of equal importance. In September, 1920, while visiting in Bath, the following incident occurred:

"One Sunday I started off in the car to go and lunch with Mrs. Knatchbull. When we had gone a few miles, however, the car broke down, a 'rubber-washer' having perished and let the water through! We telephoned for a 'Taxi' which took me back to Bath, and the car was towed back. Later in the afternoon Mrs. Knatchbull sent a car for me to go over to tea, and I flew over hill and dale and reached her place in Babington in half an hour."

So you see, the Countess really *had* intended to lunch with Mrs. Knatchbull!

We neglected to mention that the authoress is by birth a Chaplin; so she probably can get free seats whenever Mary's boy Charlie comes to town in a picture.

The Woolen Mitten
Situation

BEING A CONFIDENTIAL REPORT

*This great historical document, sometimes referred to
as the Epic of Advertising, is here presented, complete and unexpurgated, as delivered to the
A. N. A. in Atlantic City.*

I HAVE some very important data for all advertising men. I might as well admit right at the
start that my first job on leaving college was with
the advertising department of the Curtis Publishing
Co. I am probably the only ex-Curtis advertising
man who has not gone into the agency business for
himself. As a matter of fact, when I left Curtis (I
was given plenty of time to get my hat and coat)
I was advised not to stick to advertising. They
said that I was too tall, or something. I forget just
what the reason was they gave.

But one of my last jobs before leaving Curtis was
to go out on a commercial research trip for Mr.
Charles Coolidge Parlin, the well-known Curtis
commercial research sharp. Most of you have been
shown some of Mr. Parlin's reports—in strict confidence—giving you the inside dope on the distribution of your own product and proving that, by using
exclusively the Curtis publications—their names

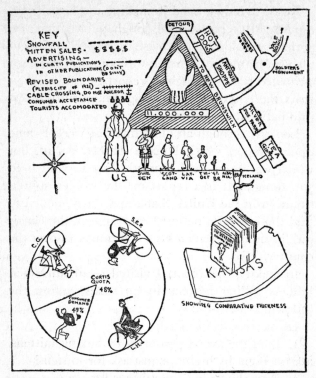

This chart shows something or other pretty graphically—we don't know just what except that Curtis is right, as usual. If the chart is correct there is certainly nothing like the Curtis Publications. At that you ought to have seen some of the dandy charts in Mr. Benchley's gingham report.

escape me at the moment—you will not only reach all the public that you want to reach but will have enough people left over to give an amateur performance of "Pinafore."

I used to have a hand in making up these Parlin reports. My report on the gingham situation was perhaps considered my most successful, owing to the neat manner in which it was bound. It has been estimated that my gingham report retarded by ten years the entrance of the gingham manufacturers into national advertising.

Looking through an old trunk last week I came upon a report which I made for Mr. Parlin, but which was never used. I would like to read it to you tonight. It is a report on the woolen mitten situation in the United States and was intended to lead the way for a national campaign in the Curtis publications to reach mitten consumers all over the country.

In making this report I visited retail stores and jobbers selling mittens in 49 states, asking the following questions:

Of the retailers I asked:

1. Does the average woman, in buying mittens, ask for them by brand or just ask for mittens?

2. Does she try on the mittens for size?

3. Is there any appreciable consumer demand for mittens during the summer? If so what the hell for?

4. Is there any appreciable consumer demand for mittens during the winter?

5. Isn't it true that a mitten with a nationally advertised trade-name—like "Mitto" or "Paddies" —provided the Curtis publications were used exclusively—would sweep the field?

6. How many mitten buyers demand that the mittens be attached together with a string?

Of the jobbers we asked the following questions:

1. How do you like jobbing?

2. Are you a college man?

3. Wouldn't you be happier doing something else?

4. Do you ever, by any chance, sell any mittens?

Out of 4,846 jobbing establishments visited, only eight jobbers were found in. Jobbing establishments are always on such dark streets and there never seems to be anybody in the store. I finally got so that I would sit in my hotel and make up the jobbers' answers myself.

Now, as a result of this investigation, the Curtis Company was able to place the following facts at the disposal of the various mitten manufacturers. Each mitten manufacturer was blindfolded and taken into a darkened room where he was made to promise that he would never tell any one the facts about his own business that he was about to be told. Then he was turned around and around until he was dizzy, and then hit over the head by the Curtis Advertising Director.

Following is the result of the mitten investigation:

1. In 49 states it was found that 615,000 women do not buy mittens at all. At first, these statistics would seem to be confusing. But, on being analyzed, it is found that 82 per cent. of these 615,000 women live in towns of a population of

50,000 or over, which means that they can keep their hands in their pockets and do not need mittens. Here, then, a consumer demand must be created.

2. From 5.6 per cent. to 95 per cent. of the department store sales of men's mittens are made to women. This just shows what we are coming to.

3. In the New England states one woman in ten buys ready-to-wear mittens instead of piece-goods from which to make her own mittens.

4. In the Middle West, one woman in eleven buys mitten piece-goods. This extra woman is accounted for by the fact that an aunt of mine went to live in Wisconsin last year.

In the South, they had never heard of mittens. At one place in Alabama we were told that they had drowned the last batch they had, thinking the inquiry had been for "kittens." This gave us an idea, and we made a supplementary report on kitten distribution. In this investigation it was found:

A. That there is no general consumer knowledge of breeds of kittens. In other words, a kitten is a kitten and that's all.

B. Four out of five kittens never do anything worthwhile in the world.

C. The market for kittens is practically negligible. In some states there are no dealers at all, and hardly any jobbers.

D. A solution of the kitten dealer-problem might lie in the introduction of dealer helps. In other words, improve the package so that the dealer can play it up. Give him a kitten he will be proud to display.

But to return to our mittens:

We have shown that a nationally advertised brand of mittens, *if* given the proper distribution and *if* adapted to the particular consumer demand in the different mitten localities throughout the country, ought to dominate the field.

We now come to the problem of the proper medium for such a campaign.

In the chart on page 299 we have a pyramid representing the Curtis circulation. Eleven million people, of whom 25,000 are able to lift the paper high enough to read it. In this shaded section here is where the country club is going to be. This is all made land. . . . We come down here to a circle showing consumer demand, 49 per cent. . . . Curtis quota 48 per cent. and here is the State of Kansas which was admitted as a free state in 1856.

To continue: in 1902, the year of the war, there were 160,000 of these sold in Michigan alone. Bring this down to present-day values, with time and a half for overtime, and you will see what I mean. Of these, 50,000 were white, 4,600 were practically white and 4,000 were the same as those in Class A—white.

We have now pretty well lined up the channels of distribution for mittens and have seen that there is only one practical method for reaching the mitten consumer, namely, 52 pages a year in the *Post*, and 12 pages in color in the *Journal* and *Country*

Gentleman. There will be no duplication here as the readers of the *Country Gentleman* go to bed so early.

In addition to the benefit derived from all this, the mitten manufacturers will be shown all over the Curtis building in Philadelphia and allowed to peek into Mr. Lorimer's office. And, if they don't like this plan for marketing their product, they can lump it, because it's all they are going to get.

This report was the start of the big campaign which put the Frivolity Mitten Co. where it is today. And, for submitting it, I was fired.

The World
of Grandpa Benchley

Thinking Out Loud in the Manner of Mr. Wells' Hero

§1

I AM eighty-nine years old, and I think I would like to write a book. I don't know—maybe I wouldn't.

§2

Eighty-nine this year, ninety next year, eighty-eight last year. That makes three years accounted for. Three into fourteen goes four times and two to carry. The Assyrians were probably the first people to evolve mathematics. I sometimes get to thinking about mathematics.

The average Englishman at the age of eighty-nine is dead—has been dead for several years. The average depth of the Caspian Sea is 3,000 feet. The average rainfall in Canada is 1.03 inches. During the Inter-Glacial Period it was 9.01 inches. Think of that—9.01 inches!

§3

All this has made me stop and think, think about the world I live in. I sometimes wonder what it is all about—this world I mean. I am not so sure about the next world. Sometimes I think there is one and sometimes I think there isn't. I'll be darned if *I* can make it out.

Grandpa Benchley

I am not so sure about my wanting to write a book, either. But something has got to be done about this world—something explanatory, I mean. Here I am, eighty-nine years old, and I haven't explained about the world to anyone yet—that is, not to anyone in this room.

§4

It is a beautiful day outside. The sun, that luminous body 95,000,000 miles from the earth, without which we should never be able to dry hides or bake biscuits, is shining through the trees outside my window, much as it used to shine through the trees outside the cave of Neolithic Man, ten thousand years before Christ. In fact, Neolithic Man sometimes built himself houses on piles driven in the water, but this was not until almost five thousand years before Christ.

Sometimes I get to thinking about Neolithic Man. Sometimes I get to thinking about Cro-Magnon Man. Sometimes it just seems as if I should go crazy thinking about things. There are so *many* things! And I am only eighty-nine.

§5

I remember when I was a very small boy my mother used to forbid me to go out when it was raining. My mother was a very quiet woman, who never spoke unless it was to figure out how long it would take to reach the nearest star by train.

"Nipper," she would say to me on such days as the rain would prevent my going out, "Nipper, I guess you don't know that thousands of years before modern civilization there was a period known as the Pluvial or Lacustrine Age, the rain or pond period."

I remember my crying myself to sleep the first night after she told me about the Pluvial or Lacustrine Age. It seemed so long ago—and nothing to be done about it.

§6

One night my father came home with a queer light in his eyes. He said nothing during dinner, except to note, as he passed me the salt, that salt is an essential to all grain-consuming and herbivorous animals but that on a meat-diet man can do without it. "There have been bitter tribal wars," he said, "between the tribes of the Soudan for possession of the salt deposits between Fezzan and Murzuk."

"Arthur," said my mother, quietly, "remember the boys are present."

"It is time they knew," was his reply.

At last my mother, sensing that something was troubling him, said:

"Arthur, are you holding something back from me?"

He laid down his knife and fork and looked at her.

"I have just heard," he said, "that the molecule is no longer the indivisible unit that it was supposed to be."

My mother bit her lip.

"You tell me this," she said, "after all these years!"

"I have just learned it myself," replied my father. "The National Molecule Society found it out themselves only last month. The new unit is to be called the 'atom.'"

"A fine time to tell me!" said my mother, her eyes blazing. "You have known it for a month."

"I wasn't sure until just now," said my father. "I didn't want to worry you."

My mother took my brother and me by the hand. "Come, boys," she said, "we are going away."

Two days later the three of us left for the Continent. We never saw my father again.

§7

This set me to thinking about atoms. I don't think that I have it straight even now. And then, just as I was getting accustomed to the idea that molecules *could* be divided into atoms, along comes somebody a few years ago and says that you can divide atoms into electrons. And, although I was about seventy-five at the time, I went out into the park and had a good cry.

I mean, what is an old fellow going to do? No sooner does he get something all thought out than something happens to make him begin all over again. I get awfully sore sometimes.

§8

Then there is this question of putting studs in a dress-shirt. Here is the problem as I see it:

If you put the studs in *before* you put the shirt on, you muss your hair putting it on over your head. If you wait until you have the shirt on before putting in the studs, you have to put your hand up under the front of the shirt and punch them through with the other. This musses the shirt bosom nine times out of ten. Eight times out of ten, perhaps.

All right. Suppose you put the studs in first and muss your hair. Then you have to brush it again. That is not so hard to do, except that if you put tonic on your hair before you brush it, as I do, you are quite likely to spatter drops down the bosom. And there you are, with a good big blister right where it shows—and it's 8 o'clock already.

Now here *is* a problem. I have spent hours trying to figure some way to get around it and am nowhere near the solution. I think I will go to the Riviera where it is quiet and just think and think and think.

§9

I am sitting at my window in the *Villa a Vendre* at Cagnes. If it were not for the Maritime Alps I could see Constantinople. How do you suppose the Alps got there, anyway? Some giant cataclysm of Nature I suppose. I guess it is too late to do anything about it now.

Irma is down in the garden gathering snails for dinner. Irma is cross at me because this morning, when she suggested running up to Paris for the shooting, I told her that the ancient name of Paris was Lutitia.

I get to thinking about women sometimes. From eight in the evening on. They are funny. Female characteristics differ so from male characteristics. This was true even in the Pleistocene Age, so they tell me.

§10

Next Wednesday I am going back to thinking about God. I didn't anywhere near finish thinking about God the last time. The man came for the trunks and I had to go with him to the station.

It is quite a problem. I don't think there is any doubt about there being some Motive Power which governs the World. But I can't seem to get much beyond that. Maybe I'll begin again on that Monday. Monday is a good day to begin thinking. Your laundry is just back and everything is sort of pristine and new. I hope that, by beginning Monday, I can get everything cleaned up by Friday, for Friday I am going over to Monte Carlo.

§11

It is six years now since I began writing this book. I am almost ninety-seven. According to the statistics of the Royal Statistical Society I can't expect much longer in which to think things over.

The big thing that is worrying me now is about putting sugar on my oatmeal. I find that if I put the sugar on first and then the cream, the sugar all disappears, and I like to see it, nice and white, there on the cereal. But if I put the cream on first and *then* the sugar, it doesn't taste so good. I asked Irma about this the other day and she told me to shut up and go back to bed.

§12

After thinking the whole thing over, I have come to the conclusion that I don't want to write a book at all. When a man is ninety-seven it is high time he was doing something else with his time besides writing books. I guess I'll go out and roll down hill.

GLOSSARY OF KIN, NATIVE, AND TECHNICAL TERMS

KIN TERMS

arndi—mother.

bapa—father.

dué—father's sister's son (husband); father's sister's daughter.

dumungur—father's sister's daughter's daughter's son; father's sister's daughter's daughter's daughter.

galle—mother's brother's son; mother's brother's daughter (wife).

gatu—son; daughter.

gawel—mother's brother.

gurrong—father's sister's daughter's son; father's sister's daughter's daughter.

kaminyer—daughter's son; daughter's daughter.

kutara—sister's daughter's son; sister's daughter's daughter.

maraitcha—son's son; son's daughter.

marelker—mother's mother's brother's son.

mari—mother's mother's brother; mother's mother.

marikmo—father's father; father's father's sister.

mokul bapa—father's sister.

mokul rumeru—mother's mother's brother's daughter (mother-in-law).

momelker—mother's mother's mother's brother's daughter.

momo—father's mother.

nati—mother's father.

natjiwalker—mother's mother's mother's brother's son.

waku—sister's son; sister's daughter; father's father's sister's son; father's father's sister's daughter.

wawa—older brother.

yeppa—sister.

yukiyuko—younger brother.

NATIVE TERMS

Bamun—the mythological period when "things were different" and the totemic spirits and the ancestors of man inhabited the land.

Bapa Indi—*see* Muit.

baperu—native name for moiety, meaning four subsections that belong to each moiety.

billibong—a general term used by the Australian whites for a small lake or pool.

bilmel, bilmal—singing sticks.

birimbir—the totemic soul of man (*see* mokoi).

corroboree—a general term used by the Australian whites for native ceremonies.

ABBREVIATIONS

A. OLD TESTAMENT

Am.	Amos	Josh.	Joshua
Cant.	Canticles (Song of Sol.)	Judg.	Judges
Chron.	Chronicles	Kings	Kings
Dan.	Daniel	Lam.	Lamentations
Deut.	Deuteronomy	Lev.	Leviticus
Eccles.	Ecclesiastes	Mal.	Malachi
Esth.	Esther	Mic.	Micah
Ex.	Exodus	Nah.	Nahum
Ez.	Ezekiel	Neh.	Nehemiah
Ezra	Ezra	Num.	Numbers
Gen.	Genesis	Obad.	Obadiah
Hab.	Habakkuk	Pr.	Proverbs
Hag.	Haggai	Ps.	Psalms
Hos.	Hosea	Ruth	Ruth
Is.	Isaiah	Sam.	Samuel
Jer.	Jeremiah	Song	Song of Songs (Cant.)
Job	Job	Zech.	Zechariah
Joel	Joel	Zeph.	Zephaniah
Jonah	Jonah		

B. NEW TESTAMENT

Acts	Acts of the Apostles	Mark	Mark
Col.	Colossians	Matt.	Matthew
Cor.	Corinthians	Pet.	Peter
Eph.	Ephesians	Phil.	Philippians
Gal.	Galatians	Philem.	Philemon
Hebr.	Hebrews	Rev.	Revelation
Jam.	James	Rom.	Romans
John	John	Thess.	Thessalonians
Jude	Jude	Tim.	Timothy
Luke	Luke	Tit.	Titus

C. APOCRYPHA

Bar.	Baruch	Macc.	Maccabees
Bel	Bel and the Dragon	Sus.	Susanna
Ecclus.	Ecclesiasticus	Tob.	Tobit
Esd.	Esdras	Wisd.	Wisdom of Solomon
Jth.	Judith	of Sol.	

BIBLIOGRAPHY

ABRAHAM, K. Selected Papers. London, Hogarth Press, 1927.

ADLER, A. The Practice and Theory of Individual Psychology. New York, Harcourt, Brace & Co., 1924.

ALEXANDER, F. The Psychoanalysis of the Total Personality. New York, Nervous and Mental Disease Pub. Co., 1930.

ALLPORT, G. W. Personality: A Psychological Interpretation. New York, Henry Holt & Co., 1937.

BAKER, H. J., and TRAPHAGEN, V. The Diagnosis and Treatment of Behavior Problem Children. New York, Macmillan Co., 1935.

BENDER, L., and BLAU, A. Reaction of children to sexual relations with adults. Am. J. Orthopsychiat., 7: 500-518, 1937.

BOLLES, M. M., and ZUBIN, J. A graphic method for evaluating differences between frequencies. J. Applied Psychology, 23: 440-449, 1939.

BREUER, J., and FREUD, S. Studien über Hysterie. Leipzig, F. Deuticke, 1895.

BROMLEY, D. D., and BRITTEN, F. H. Youth and Sex. New York, Harper & Brothers, 1938.

BURGESS, E. W., and COTTRELL, L. S., JR. Predicting Success or Failure in Marriage. New York, Prentice-Hall, Inc., 1939.

CALDWELL, W. E., and MOLOY, H. C. Anatomical variations in the female pelvis and their effect in labor with a suggested classification. Am. J. Obst. & Gynec., 26: 479-505, 1933.

CALDWELL, W. E., MOLOY, H. C., and D'ESOPO, D. A. Further studies on the pelvic architecture. Am. J. Obst. & Gynec., 28: 482-497, 1934.

CHENEY, C. O. Outlines for Psychiatric Examination. Utica, State Hospitals Press, 1934.

DAVIS, K. B. Factors in the Sex Life of Twenty-Two Hundred Women. New York, Harper & Brothers, 1929.

DICKINSON, R. L. Human Sex Anatomy. Baltimore, Williams and Wilkins, 1933.

DICKINSON, R. L., and BEAM, L. A Thousand Marriages. Baltimore, Williams & Wilkins Co., 1931.

DICKINSON, R. L., and BEAM, L. The Single Woman. Baltimore, Williams & Wilkins Co., 1934.

DIETHELM, O. Treatment in Psychiatry. New York, Macmillan Co., 1936.

ELLIS, H. Studies in the Psychology of Sex. Ed. 3. Philadelphia, F. A. Davis Co., 1910. Vol. 1.

Index